WILL YOU PRAY WITH ME

This book is dedicated to my husband, Eric.
Thank you for your love and support.
—Anne

To my wife, Karen,
who has always encouraged me to write this book.
—Steve

Steve Langhofer and Anne Williams

WILL YOU
PRAY
WITH ME

A Guide for Those
Who Pray in Public

Abingdon Press
Nashville

WILL YOU PRAY WITH ME:
A GUIDE FOR THOSE WHO PRAY IN PUBLIC

Copyright © 2021 by Abingdon Press

Library of Congress Control Number: 2021942002

ISBN: 978-1-7910-1343-1

Scripture quotations unless noted otherwise are taken from the Common English Bible, copyright 2011.
Used by permission. All rights reserved. www.CommonEnglishBible.com.

21 22 23 24 25 26 27 28 29 30—10 9 8 7 6 5 4 3 2 1
MANUFACTURED IN THE UNITED STATES OF AMERICA

Contents

Contents

Preface

It is odd to write a book on prayer. Praying is such an extraordinarily personal endeavor. Never would I ever want to dictate someone else's conversation with God, nor would I want to make it seem like there is a right and a wrong way to pray. God delights in raw, unrefined, well-intended prayers—maybe even more than well-planned, well-executed prayers. The problem isn't that there is something wrong with your prayers or that you need to fix them.

The problem is that there are pastors who are new to this work and are in search of a little guidance. There are pastors who graduated seminary and landed in their first church realizing they barely got one lesson on how to lead a congregation in prayer. Then there are pastors who are not new to this work but who feel a little burned out. There are also pastors who spend their time focused on preaching, stewardship campaigns, pastoral care, or a million other tasks; crafting a pastoral prayer is always the least prioritized item on the to-do list.

Then there are lay people who are called to serve but feel ill-prepared. They teach Sunday school, direct the choir, fold bulletins, or even unclog the toilet. But if you dare ask for a volunteer to lead in a closing prayer they break out into a cold sweat. They will absolutely avoid eye contact from across the table, hoping (praying?) they aren't called upon. They feel unworthy or unqualified in some way. They have perfectly vibrant prayer lives and yet leading a group in prayer is a whole different venture.

I (Anne) always deal with a certain level of anxiety around any type of public "speaking." Public prayer, holy as it is, is not exempt. Still to this day, my heart pounds, my armpits sweat, and I feel like I could throw up every single time. Sometimes my knees even weaken and my hands shake. I find that the more I care about the content I am presenting, the more nervous I am. If you feel sick when you step forward to lead, know that you are not alone.

—Anne Williams

I (Steve) have long been in love with the process of writing and sharing prayers. My love of it started surprisingly early. During the spring of my senior year in high school I took part in a week-long biology field trip to Florida. About forty of us packed into a bus and every day was an adventure full of discovery. The day before we were to return home my teacher asked if I would offer a prayer at the evening campfire. I had never prayed in public, nor did I have much knowledge of the religious inclination of my classmates. I found the challenge daunting and irresistible.

I spent hours putting that small prayer together, all the time questioning my adequacy. I began making a list of trip highlights, bus conversations, and the new friendships being nurtured. I included countryside hikes in quest of novel plant and animal species, science museum explorations, collecting seashells and driftwood. I also wrote down the boat ride with a fishing haul of water critters that I wanted to investigate, my first taste of Southern grits, and even tree frogs serenading under moonlit skies.

My prayer became a simple litany of communal thanksgiving. (It is never a mistake to begin prayer with gratitude.) I, who initially shuddered to address God on behalf of others, managed sufficiently. It was a decent prayer. To my amazement I unearthed a keen eagerness to do it again.

I am still doing it, over fifty years later. I am still in love with the process of writing and sharing. It has become easier, more natural. I dream that through this book my enthusiasm becomes contagious. If I could learn how to write and share prayers in public, and delight in the process, then so can you!

—Steve Langhofer

Together, our hope is that this book can guide prayer-writing and prayer-offering that changes the religious landscape of our future. We hope that more people will come to know the grace of God, the unconditional, sacrificial love of Jesus, and the fruit of the Holy Spirit.

INTRODUCTION

Public Prayer Is Not the Same as Private Prayer

I (Anne) have offered a fair number of prayers in my short career as a pastor, mostly because as an associate pastor, the pastoral prayer tends to be one of the primary ways I end up leading in a Sunday morning worship service. And even still, there are times that I sit down to begin and all I see is a blank screen and a blinking cursor, and feel absolutely no inspiration. In pulling together prayers from the past few years for this book, more than once I would open up a document expecting to find a written prayer only to find nothing but a half-sentence. I don't have record of why it was left incomplete. Did an emergency phone call interrupt me? Did I end up writing something out with pen and paper? Did I wing it? Was I busy with other tasks, or just feeling solidly uninspired? It's not particularly hard to pray to God when it's just me and God. But when you add in the hundred other elements involved in public prayer, it gets really overwhelming really quickly. What is it about praying in public that is so intimidating?

Terrible moments of public prayer make for great comedic film. If you've seen *Meet the Fockers* or *Talladega Nights*, you already know what I'm talking about. It is painful, and also hysterical, to watch someone offer a prayer that so misses the mark. In *National Lampoon's Christmas Vacation*, the family is seated at the formal dining room table for the long-awaited Christmas meal. Anticipation is at a peak, and everyone is ready to dig in when eighty-year-old Aunt Bethany is invited to offer a blessing over the dinner. After everyone folds their hands and bows their heads, ready to recognize the bounty of God's grace and provision, she begins, "I pledge allegiance to the flag . . ."

You're not likely to recite The Pledge of Allegiance accidentally, but what if you were to pray something shallow or boring or weird? What if you were to stumble, stutter, or freeze up? What if you were to say something offensive or off-putting? What had been so deeply personal between you and God is now placed under a spotlight on a stage. It would be like having your personal journals on display for everyone to read. Though it isn't a performance, it is public leadership. We are vulnerable and exposed. Our people are listening. First-time guests are paying attention. Leading public prayer is not as simple as taking your personal prayer life and sharing it with a group. Others will be in the room with us, experiencing the prayer, and it is our responsibility to consider their experience. Our hope is that this book can help guide you to adjust your prayer-writing from a personal relationship between you and God to focus on worship leadership in a group setting.

Giving and Receiving Mentorship, Passing It On

I (Anne) have learned a lot over ten years, thanks to the guidance of mentors and colleagues who have shaped my approach over the course of time. None of what I offer in this book is my own. I have received so much guidance and internalized it to the point I can no longer decisively identify which nuggets came from whom.

I do know I was forced by Brian to preach my first sermon at church camp as a teenager. I was beyond reluctant. (This is all your fault, Brian.) Then, of course, Brian introduced me to the one and only Gayla who changed my life with the mentorship she has given me and the way she still pours wisdom and grace into me to this day. Gayla's ability to make theology come alive inspires me to find common words for deep concepts. Her quick wit reminds me that it is good to laugh during worship and we don't have to take ourselves so seriously. I admired the positivity and sincere, unconditional love Wendy offered her congregation. Her prayers ooze with compassion and empathy, helping worshippers to feel at ease. Glen taught me to believe in what I had on the paper but to lead with conviction and passion. He believed in my call on days when I felt like I couldn't go on. Scott has challenged me to be myself unapologetically, to own my voice, and to teach out of my own authentic life experience. He thrust me into opportunities that I would have never known to ask for and laid out a path for me to grow my leadership. Congregants have complimented and critiqued along the way. Some comments helped me refine my work. Other comments didn't serve a constructive purpose, and I had to let them go.

I hope to take all these pieces and boil them together to offer my best to God and those I am entrusted to serve. Pastoral work is so much better when we have companions for the journey. We need to be mentors ourselves as much as we need to receive mentoring, and the very best set-up is when we get to be on both the giving and receiving ends in the same season. We are never too experienced to learn something new, and there are always newbies coming up behind us who can use a word of encouragement. I hope the guidance Steve and I offer in the pages to come feels like a friendly mentor coming alongside you as we fine-tune our craft together. I hope you feel the spirit of a long line of guides that have nurtured and assisted me in becoming who I am and praying the way I pray.

A Future Church

We sit firmly in an era marked by the decline of religious practice in America. More and more people are disaffiliating with organized religion. From 2009–2019 the Pew Research Center found that the percentage of Americans who describe themselves as Christian fell from 77 percent to 65 percent. Even more pertinent to the conversation on leading public prayer is how often Americans find themselves sitting in a church service, participating in a pastoral prayer. "Over the last decade, the share of Americans who say they attend religious services at least once or twice a month dropped by 7 percentage points, while the share who say they attend religious services less often (if at all) has risen by the same degree." Fifty-four percent of Americans say they attend a religious service "a few times a year or less."[1] We have fewer and fewer opportunities throughout the year to make an impression with those who might be on the fence about church engagement in coming weeks. If we have any power to reverse this trend, leveraging the power of the pastoral prayer will be part of the solution.

I think about future generations, and I desperately want my children to have thoughtful, engaging church services available to show up to. I want them to experience something in church that feels so helpful and so needed that they can't get it anywhere else and their life depends on being in church services. Fantastic sermons and powerful worship music are available on demand through podcasts and streaming services. They can be accessed with the click of a mouse during someone's commute, while they're folding laundry, or any other time that is convenient. Pastoral prayer is a holy moment that can't be replicated at home. What would it be like if future generations woke up on Sunday morning, and while deciding if they wanted to attend a worship service or not, they were struck with a memory from the last time they were in church and a pastoral prayer stirred their heart and brought them a sense of peace amid the storms of life. What if they wanted to go back because something the pastor said in that prayer made them feel understood? What if they longed for Sunday morning services all through the week because something offered in the prayer time removed the stigma out of acknowledging doubts or fears or laments? What if the time of silent confession is exactly what they needed to begin the week with a clean slate and reset their devotion to following Christ? I have a vision of pastoral prayer being one mark of revitalization in the mainline church. We too easily miss a chance to connect, to teach, to inspire with the prayer. When the pastoral prayer misses the mark, it is nothing more than a chance to get in a quick catnap as we shut our eyes for a moment or make a grocery list, while the pastor drones on using religious jargon that wastes our time.

How can we make a time of pastoral prayer irresistible? Most Americans still seek connection with God even in their disaffiliation with organized religion. Striking research shows that 54 percent of what Pew calls "Religious Resisters" talk to God.[2] This "talking to God" is common ground to build upon, an opportunity to connect through prayer. It is an opportunity to be the church in the best possible way, filled with grace and mercy rather than the shame and guilt that is often associated with religion.

In my experience at a vibrant urban Methodist church in Kansas City, Missouri, churchgoers return to church when they see there is a place where their questions are welcomed, unconditional love is not only preached but also lived out, and participants are invited to join a journey of growing together rather than expected to blindly follow. They are attracted to faith that is more nuanced than black and white, and Christian discipleship is more about submitting our lives to God than about rules and right answers. Together we work on expanding our idea of God and practice receiving a love that is so unimaginable it can be sometimes hard to internalize. Many of our church members would have recently called themselves "religious resisters" or religiously unaffiliated not because they didn't want to have a relationship with God but because the church as a whole or Christians specifically had caused harm. They heard the message that they aren't good enough, they aren't holy enough, and God's love isn't for them (at least not until they change into something different). Shame and guilt drove their experience of organized religion. Can you think of the amazing power a pastoral prayer has to shift a person's experience of religion? The right words, the right tone, the right intention can feel like the Prodigal Father's warm embrace when his child returns home.

Let's zoom out for a moment and recognize that even nonreligious Americans do set foot in churches at other times, namely for weddings and funerals. These events are some of church's best evangelism opportunities. We see people enter the doors of a church who otherwise would not. Who knows what they expect to find! In the case of a memorial service, acquaintances of the deceased approach the doors of the sanctuary looking for a service that honors the life of their friend or neighbor or colleague. In the case of the closest family members to the deceased, they enter often broken open, overwhelmed by grief, and in need of solace. In the case of a wedding, it's a joyful, celebratory occasion where the service of worship is sometimes given very little thought compared to the party that will follow. Regardless of what attendees expect, we have a say in what they find. Imagine if they walk away surprised! Imagine if there is something spoken there that stops them in their tracks—powerful, life-giving, cup-filling. Imagine if there was something uttered in a prayer that made them feel understood on a spiritual level, filling a void they didn't even know was there. What if it was relatable? What if theological concepts were communicated in a way that made them approachable and memorable? What if there was something about those services that made attendees say to themselves, "What was the name of that church again? I wonder when their weekend services are. . . ." And quickly we can see that to have our heartstrings tugged in these types of situations may begin to move the needle for the future of our church.

My hope is that this book can guide prayer-writing and prayer-praying that changes the religious landscape of our future, so that more people know the grace of God, the unconditional, sacrificial love of Jesus, and the fruit of the Holy Spirit.

Introduction

If you have doubted your ability to lead people in prayer, this book is for you. If your weeks are frenzied and you do not have time to compose expected prayers, this book is for you. Perhaps you are mentally exhausted, and inspiration escapes you. Whether you are a beginner or a veteran pray-er, immersing yourself in these pages should prove beneficial.

Part One

PRINCIPLES, PREPARATION, AND DELIVERY

CHAPTER ONE

Guiding Principles for Prayer-Writing

1. Begin with Christ

How does one best begin writing? Start with a posture of humility. Light a candle. Seek the mind of Christ. Pray to be ushered into the mystery of co-creating with God, a grace-filled process surpassing our understanding. Acknowledge this as a holy privilege to which God has called us.

We need an initial idea. Perhaps we feel richly blessed, so we start there. Perhaps a current event dominates the weekly news, and we begin there. Sometimes a neighbor is struggling with depression, a loved one is seriously ill, a dear friend dies, and we find it hard to think about anything else. Sometimes we don't have a clue. A beginning point is imperative.

All too often we enter the composition process feeling uncertain where to start. It helps to offer a prayer something like this:

> *Jesus, help me know where to start. Help me remember my experiences of this week and the insights You've given me. Help me imagine myself standing before Your altar table, lifting to You the joys and concerns of the ones I've encountered. Put me in touch again with their heartaches, their happiness. Reveal to me what You would have me say on their behalf. Please, Holy Spirit, show me the way.*

We receive great comfort in remembering we never craft our pastoral prayers alone. We have a Helpmate (John 14:16-17, 26), an Advocate when we don't know what to pray.

3

When we labor diligently on our prayers, occasionally following worship someone will express appreciation. We are wise to simply smile and quietly thank them. We can take appropriate pride in the results of our labor, all the time remembering it was not our own doing. Mostly we are proud of God who provided every word that came out of our mouths and who promised they would not return empty (Isa 55:11). We are proud of God who refuses to be God apart from us, who uses us to continue creating something out of nothing (John 14:12). What amazing grace! And most amazing of all is that we get to be part of it!

> *Thank You, O God, for being You, and for loving us the way You do. Make us who lead others in prayer worthy not only of praying to You, but also for Your daughters and sons. Keep speaking. We'll keep listening. Keep giving us Your words of grace and truth, accomplishing far more than we could ask or imagine.*

2. Write Out the Prayer

Coming up with prayers is a labor of love. It doesn't always come easily, and it can seem to take too long. Some days we think, "I don't have time to write out my prayer. I'll just wing it and trust the guidance of the Holy Spirit." Yes, Jesus did counsel us not to worry beforehand about our words when called upon to speak publicly, that God's spirit would provide (Mark 13:11). But he was talking about crisis situations demanding an immediate proclamation of the gospel. Normally we are not under such pressure. We have time to reflect and choose words carefully.

We want to present the very best expressions possible, demonstrating our love of God with heart, soul, strength, and *mind*! Why would we settle for less? This requires deliberate, thorough preparation. To write out a prayer ahead of time doesn't mean we cannot still deliver it from memory. But the advanced groundwork may well produce a prayer of greater excellence and beauty.

Writing our prayer in advance helps keep us within appropriate time limitations whether in worship, during a meeting, or at a hospital bedside. It also gives us the assurance we won't forget something we really want to say. Making time to write a priority is well worth our effort.

3. Know Your Goal

Before you begin, you must know why you're doing what you're doing. There are so many ways that a prayer time can be used. Keep your goal in mind to remain focused and deliberate. You'll waste less time and reach a more satisfying conclusion this way.

It is most useful to take time with this question yourself, to determine what you must accomplish by leading your community in prayer, especially if it is a role that you will be occupying for any length of time, or with regularity. Some questions to consider are: Why is a prayer time included in your worship service at all? and What do you feel God is calling you to do with this opportunity?

After some consideration, your answers to these questions will guide you in moments when you are stuck, moments where you are forced to make difficult decisions about what to include or not include. Your thoughtful preparation will ultimately help your congregation feel led with clear direction. In any case, no matter what your goal is, a few things are certain. Your goal is *not* to sit on a high horse of religiosity and show your community how holy you are. Your goal is *not* to shame or guilt others through prayer. You goal is *not* to preach a mini-sermon. Your goal is *not* to bring an agenda and manipulate others to fall in line with the leader. Your goal is *never* to misrepresent God or create a stumbling block in someone else's faith life.

Here's something to consider as part of your discernment: the leader of public prayer facilitates a conversation between the group and God. You are tasked with the remarkable privilege of giving voice to those praying along with you.

So, what *is* your goal as the one offering a public prayer on behalf of a gathered group? One possible response is: **Your goal as a prayer leader is to facilitate a conversation between the group and God**. Your goal is to help your community put words to what they are feeling about their faith life. Maybe you help them move forward by offering a bit of a challenge, or by voicing a thought or phrase that creates the space for a thoughtful pause. A little nudging, from time to time, is helpful.

More often than not, especially in the context of a worship service, your goal is to **represent the community to God, lifting the prayers of the**

5

people. You offer to God words that convey the thoughts and feelings of the people who are gathered, their burdens and joys. When our pastoral prayers achieve this goal, congregants are able to connect with God more fully. They might think to themselves, "I have been feeling that exact thing, but I didn't know how to express it to God!" What an opportunity we have to facilitate people's honest self-expression to God, allowing them to voice lament, doubt, or fear.

In *Life Together*, the Lutheran pastor, Dietrich Bonhoeffer, wrote about the importance of one person praying for others in Christian community:

> It is his [her] responsibility to pray for the fellowship. So he will have to share the daily life of the fellowship; he must know the cares, the needs, the joys and thanksgivings, the petitions and hopes of the others. Their work and everything they bring with them must not be unknown to him. He prays as a brother among brothers. It will require practice and watch-fulness, if he is not to confuse his own heart with the heart of the fellowship, if he is really to be guided solely by his responsibility to pray for the fellowship.[1]

Another possible response is: **your goal as a prayer leader is to help prepare the congregation to hear the message of the sermon or experience the remaining elements of the worship service**. Perhaps a confession is necessary, or perhaps the congregation can't make room for more information or teaching until they know God has heard and received whatever concerns they walked into the sanctuary carrying. The prayer, then, is an opportunity to release and surrender those burdens and create space in the spirit for whatever is to be received by later elements of worship. In this situation, you think of the prayer as one element of a larger worship arc. That arc is heading in a particular direction and the prayer plays a specific role in building the desired experience throughout the hour of corporate worship.

It is important to remember that each different prayer assignment has its own context. The group's needs and your goal for leading them in prayer will require revaluation. Each time you sit down before an open journal or a blank document to craft a prayer is a chance to pause, reflect, and remember why you are leading this community in prayer.

4. Imagine God's Perspective

We must keep the needs of our hearers in mind, along with our goal for the prayer. But it is also important as we prepare a prayer to try as best as we can to view the task from God's perspective. What concerns God—in the world and in this community of people? Where is God present in small moments and in massive sweeps of time, and how might our prayer reconnect people with God by recalling those moments? These four habits can help us imagine God's perspective:

Stay Tuned to What's Going on in the World. What is being reported in the news? Have there been tragedies? What are the current controversies? We hope to learn from as many perspectives as possible about what people might bring with them into the sanctuary. Try to imagine what breaks God's heart as God watches over us as we pursue our self-centered agendas or drive our lives into a ditch.

What meetings did we attend this week? What topics might hold relevance to daily living, such as church finances, children's ministry, recovery support groups, mission trips, marches for social justice, or a special worship service for senior adults living with dementia? Always keep listening to those speaking, to our own thoughts and feelings, and to God's still small voice (1 Kgs 19:12).

Practice. It takes time to develop these habits. Be patient with yourself.

Pay Attention. The potential sources that shape a pastoral prayer are limitless. My father (Steve) used to say, "Son, you'll learn something every day if you pay attention!" We miss too much. We cannot include everything every time. Great lines we are proud of writing end up on the cutting-room floor, saved for another week perhaps. That is why we keep files.

Regularly Read the Psalms. This is the great prayer book of our spiritual ancestors, a remarkable window into God's eternal presence in the world. For good reason, Jesus memorized these prayers. They are useful for us in prayer-writing, too. We can imagine, for instance, how we might work the opening verses of Psalm 139 into our prayer: "O gracious Lord, You have searched us thoroughly. You understand us better than we'll ever understand ourselves. You know our thoughts, our ambitions, our worries and fears."

Or apply Psalm 51: "Have mercy upon us, O God. As we open our hearts before You, receive our confessions. Wash us. Cleanse us from our sins. Forgive us when we miss the mark." Why not borrow thoughts from some of the greatest prayers ever written, paraphrasing them into our own words, words God can use and that people can grasp?

Keep a Prayer Journal. This is a mechanism for you to invite, and listen to, God's voice intentionally. It is an opportunity to discern God's perspective. Write your own prayer concerns, bits of prayer, full-length litanies—whatever resonates with you. Include things that move you to tears of sadness or joy. If you gain a new self-awareness, write it down. If God surprises you with an experience or an idea, that goes in. Sometimes a particular word, phrase, or sentence is given to us. Try always to anchor journal entries with a scripture reference that keeps you humble and connected to our tradition. We are not the first to walk these valleys and plateaus.

5. Understand the People and the Setting

To write a meaningful prayer you must know your audience and the situation they are in. Of course, your prayers will be written out of your own experience, but this book specifically addresses the task of leading a corporate prayer. This requires thoughtful consideration of context and people in the room.

Many of you are charged with writing and leading pastoral prayers for corporate worship in a local church, so the answer may seem obvious. But you must dig a little deeper: Who are they? What jobs do they occupy? What is their home life like? What is their faith background? What is their biblical literacy like? What challenges do they face in daily life?

To go even deeper, create mock profiles of imaginary people you will be leading in prayer. One might be a single mom with two young children at home, working a minimum-wage job and looking worn out when she walks into the sanctuary Sunday morning. She is questioning her faith and whether she believes in God, but it is well worth her time to have an hour of quiet. Plus, her children beg her to come to Sunday school each week. Another one might be a recently retired executive and top dog in town. He touts that he is excited for his frequent tee times at the local country club but, underneath it all, he is scared of a new routine and questioning his identity now that his career has come to an end. Make a few profiles of your own. Name them. Imagine them coming into worship, ardently seeking connection with the divine. For what do they need you to pray? How can you offer a prayer that nurtures and guides them into an honest self-expression to God, rather than lulls them to sleep?

You may be called to write and lead prayer for other settings as well. The audiences at a recovery center, high school commencement ceremony, civic community event, youth group, or a third-grade Sunday school class are distinct from one another. Do your best to understand these people and their needs, and to cater your prayer to them specifically. Do a bit of research if necessary. Make a phone call or send a few emails. The minimal time you spend will be remarkably helpful. You'll learn to "read the room" before you're even in the room. Once you have a basic understanding of the people and the situation, you'll be able to discern how best to lead them in prayer. When people arrive at this event or in this setting, what will they be thinking, feeling? What stressors will they bring in the room with them? What connection to faith will they have? How will they feel about a prayer being offered at all? The more you can put yourselves into the shoes of your audience, the greater the chance you will offer a prayer that reflects the hearts of those on whose behalf you pray.

Once you've begun to understand the people and the setting, you can begin to zero in on the prayer itself. Consider these questions:

What kinds of language would it be best to use? Be intentional about the vocabulary you use. Even if you have a theological term in mind that would be perfect to use, avoid it at all costs. Your seminary professor would be impressed, but everyone else will be zoning out. (Except in the case of leading a prayer for your local seminary's weekly worship service, perhaps.) Instead, keep the intention of that thought. Define it, use a layman's description of that same concept and people will jump on board immediately. Use a thesaurus if you need to. It's not cheating, it's using your resources! The word *sanctification*, for example, feels haughty and overly religious. *Transformation*, on the other hand, is relatable and approachable. (We will cover word choice in greater detail in subsequent chapters.)

What would be tone-deaf or off-putting? What would make the whole room cringe, if you were to mention it? At the graveside service of a congregant who passed away of a heart attack, don't pray a line about how "we are heart-sick over the grief that we face . . ." When leading a worship service at the local dementia care facility, where most residents are confined to a wheelchair, avoid using phrases in your prayer like "Give us courage to stand up for what we believe in . . ." Context matters and what works in some situations will absolutely fail in others!

It hurts when we get this wrong. I (Anne) was officiating the memorial service of a young man who had passed away tragically and unexpectedly. From my time spent with the family prior to the service, I knew they were distraught that their loved one had not been baptized. Yet, there I stood, ill-prepared, when I began to read the United Methodist prayer traditionally offered at the graveside:

> As in baptism *Name* put on Christ,
> so in Christ may *Name* be clothed with glory.[2]

The implication in this prayer was that this man, their deceased beloved, would only gain access to heavenly glory *if* he'd been baptized. I had no intention of leading a prayer or guiding a service that would create concern about his entrance into eternal life with Christ. My hope, in fact, had been to offer peace, comfort, and grace. But my words were careless. I simply took the script I was accustomed to using, and cut and pasted it into my script for this particular occasion. Even if you are reusing prayers that you have prayed many other times in many other situations, I caution you to avoid cutting and pasting. Read through the words. Think about the words. Your context matters.

If your prayer indicates that you understand your audience and your setting, this is a sign of respect and thoughtfulness. By considering the people you serve, you are meeting folks where they are. That doesn't mean you have to pretend to be them. We don't recommend acting like a third-grader if you are praying with third-graders in Sunday school. You don't have to pretend to be something you're not. Instead, your role is to show that you know and understand whom you are praying with and to adjust your practices to meet the needs of those you serve.

6. Prepare Well but Allow the Spirit to Agitate You

Much of this chapter has focused on how to prepare great prayers. Preparation is an important part of the process! Great prayer is usually the result of thoughtfulness, prayer, intentionality, and work put in ahead of time.

That being said, the Holy Spirit doesn't always work on a schedule. Have you ever walked up to a chancel and looked down at a prepared script and felt this nudge? You know the nudge: it's a gnawing feeling, a stirring that urges you to abandon ship. You may feel like ripping your notes out of your folder and shredding them on the spot. You may not have any idea why, just an intuition. That is enough. Allow the spirit to lead.

Or maybe a congregant said something to you in the narthex before service. Their comment sparked an idea or gave you a flash of insight. Maybe you woke up to a friend's text message that made you see something in a new light or gave you verbiage for something that had previously been unspoken. Maybe some sort of news story hit after you sent your notes to the printer. Make space for the spirit to speak. It is A-OK to save what you wrote for another time; to trash it completely; or to mark it up like mad trying to salvage what you can, yet staying flexible to the changing tide. It is OK to admit to your congregation, "I had something else planned but at the last moment I decided to change directions."

We might take a cue from Jesus's response to interruption while he is on an important and urgent mission to raise a synagogue leader's daughter back to life (Mark 5:22). We find him heading in a perfectly good direction. He is heading to provide healing and hope, to show God's great power and might to the nation. But then, he gets a feeling, and is willing to stop and notice. Jesus takes a moment to look around at that courageous woman who reached out and touched the hem of his garment. I wouldn't blame him if he were annoyed. But the Spirit moved and Jesus allowed Himself to change His course. He welcomed a new idea. And that woman's life was forever changed, to say nothing of the lives changed by her subsequent witness.

11

7. Know the God to Whom You Pray

Just before giving us the words of The Lord's Prayer in the Gospel of Matthew, Jesus provides some clear—and rather firm—instruction for prayer. He guides his listeners toward private prayer over corporate prayer. He suggests that the best setting for prayer is isolation, secrecy, and seclusion. He says, "When you pray, don't be like hypocrites. They love to pray standing in the synagogues and on the street corners so that people will see them. I assure you, that's the only reward they'll get. But when you pray, go to your room, shut the door, and pray to your Father who is present in that secret place. Your Father who sees what you do in secret will reward you" (Matt 6:5-6).

What do we make, then, of our role as a prayer leader in public settings? How can we be public prayer leaders without becoming hypocrites? How do we seek a reward from God in heaven, rather than public appreciation and applause? This teaching reminds us of the character of the God to whom we pray. Prayer, like the rest of worship, is not a performance. Our prayers are a humble offering to God.

God, The Focus of Our Prayer

What complicates this is the reality of praying before a group: knowing that others are listening, that some might be judging, and that people are using your content and material to try to engage with God. Our work must be done in a public setting, even though Jesus was clear that the most honest, humble, gracious way to pray was in secrecy, when no one was watching. Praying to God, in front of other people, with other people's best interest in mind is a complicated thing.

Paul's words in the first chapter of his letter to the Galatians inspire and embolden us not to seek human approval. After all, it is God's grace that saves us: "Am I trying to win over human beings or God? Or am I trying to please people? If I were still trying to please people, I wouldn't be Christ's slave. Brothers and sisters, I want you to know that the gospel I preached isn't human in origin. I didn't receive it or learn it from a human. It came through a revelation from Jesus Christ" (Gal 1:10-12).

God, Who Is Neither Impressed nor Deceived

Even when our focus is rightly on God, it is tempting to use public prayer as a way of acting good for God. It is tempting to put on airs and project a faith that might not accurately represent our true reality. While our intentions in doing so might be pure-hearted, in that we want to give our best to God, God cannot be deceived. God already knows how we're *really* doing. God already knows where we have failed. God already knows our struggle to be completely trusting and to give our lives fully away in sacrificial love. Perhaps the most pleasing prayer for God to hear is the one with honest, heartfelt words that are simply put without pretense or formality. God longs for us to come clean and wants our true heart. God wants our honest and authentic joy, sorrow, frustration, questions, and our desperate need for saving. To fake a prayer before God is disappointing, but to fake a prayer before God and a community of people is misleading and is a misuse of power. Don't project a spotless faith that never fails and never strays. That unrealistic faith creates shame and guilt in the people sitting in our pews, something the church needs no more of. Plus, God never asked for our perfection, only our honest, contrite hearts.

We are not trying to pray well to impress our God. A beautifully crafted, eloquently spoken prayer can be a wonderful expression of deep faith. It can be a statement of love for God and a transforming channel through which God's spirit moves and brings new life. But none of it is for the purpose of earning what has already been bought for us. Bad prayers don't upset God and good prayers don't earn God's favor.

God, The Object of Our Gratitude

One of my (Anne's) favorite opening lines to a prayer is "Thank you for waking us up." We take waking up for granted most days, so it may seem like an odd object of gratitude. But to thank God for waking us up recognizes that we do take it for granted—we take life for granted. It acknowledges that someone, somewhere *didn't* wake up this morning, that someone, somewhere found a loved one who didn't wake up. It is grim to think about, but also it acknowledges the miracle right in front of our eyes. It's another day to receive God's grace, another day to use what I've been given to serve God. I have another day to try my best, learn, and grow! Thank you, God.

God, Who Hears Us

Finally, we serve a God who promises to hear the cries of His people. Time and time again, throughout the stories of Israel and the message of Jesus, we hear testimony of a God who remembers His flock, a God who hears their cry, and a God who cares for their well-being. The pastor of my childhood, the Reverend Laurence Jay Greenwood, ended every one of his sermons by saying ". . . because at the heart of things there is a God who cares." And that statement of faith is at the heart of our prayer life, as well. We pray because there is a God who listens when we do so, and a God who cares about what we say: "When you call me and come and pray to me, I will listen to you. When you search for me, yes, search for me with all your heart, you will find me" (Jer 29:12-13).

Not only did God create us and set this world into motion, not only did God promise to stick with us and redeem and restore every last one of us, God also promises to care. He promises to listen and to care about every one of His children, to hear their gratitude, hopes, longings, suffering and pain, and their questions and doubts. What a privilege it is to help others approach this God as we lead and guide them in prayer.

Develop Your Theology of Prayer

That being said, just because God is endlessly faithful in *hearing* our prayer and *caring* about our prayer, not all prayers are answered, and definitely not always the way we want them to be answered. What does prayer do, then? Does prayer bring about world peace? Does it produce food for starving children across the globe? Does it give the addict freedom from the desire to drink? Does prayer even work?

Absolutely! I (Anne) could tell you story after story of individuals who have experienced a life change because of prayer. As pastors, we have the amazing privilege of hearing these stories when they occur. In my own life, I witnessed the power of prayer to heal my first son after he suffered a stroke during his birth. He was rushed into the neonatal intensive care unit of the hospital after he began having seizures and briefly stopped breathing—on the first day of his life. We learned he had endured a stroke and were told we would have to "wait and see" if he would ever walk, talk, or go to school. Immediately, people began praying. I can't even tell you how many people prayed or how far the concern stretched. But friends called friends who put his name on prayer chains all over the world, and God began hearing about this little infant who needed help.

I will never cease being grateful that those prayers worked. Our son made a miraculous recovery and now leads a completely normal life. He has never needed extra therapies or interventions to grow and develop on a healthy timetable.

If you ask my father-in-law about this, he will tell you about the moment he was there in the hospital room holding my son in his arms. Frequently, the monitors would start beeping to report that one of his vital signs was of concern. A nurse would come check on him any time this happened. As Tom was holding him, softly but firmly, he uttered a prayer to God asking that God would watch over this child. At that instant an energy came through him and through his arms to the child. It was a calm energy but unmistakable. Instantly my father-in-law began to cry. My mother-in-law asked what was going on and he said, "The Lord just touched JD." Several minutes later, the doctor came by. He looked at the monitors, looked at the chart, and looked back at the monitors. Then he turned to the nurse and said, "What is going on? They don't match." Tom spoke up, "The Lord just touched him." The doctor replied, "Praise God! This happens more than you know." Shortly thereafter, my son was discharged from the hospital and ready to thrive at home.

We truly have a story of healing and hope to share with the world, and we have been doing so ever since. His whole life is a testimony. But I struggle when some respond to his recovery by exclaiming, "It is because so many people were praying for him!" All I can think is about the many, many children who have encountered health concerns, who have had loads of prayers sent up on their behalf, yet ended up with a different outcome. A pit of survivor's guilt churns in my stomach.

Why was my child spared and another was not? Were there not *enough* people praying for that other child? Were the prayers not as good quality, somehow? If they had prayed just one more time, or ten minutes longer, would their wish have come true? Of course that's not how God works, especially in the case of innocent children!

How do we make sense of this? Does prayer change God's mind about a situation? If so, why sometimes yes, but other times no? You have felt this tension before.

Prayer is not a magic wand. It is not a vending machine. It is not a tool that we use to acquire what we want. What *does* prayer do? This is so incredibly tricky; it is, perhaps, the hardest theological concept to wrestle with on a day-to-day basis. It is also one of the most common, and one of the most personal.

There are a couple factors at play here. First, faith life is not about enjoying more convenience. No one signs up to follow Christ hoping that doing so will make their life easier. At least, Christ never promised that. In fact, to his first followers, Christ guaranteed strife, complications, and suffering.

In the Gospel of John, Jesus goes so far as to warn his disciples: "in the world you have distress" (John 16:33). Perhaps some of that warning was particular to their context, living in a first-century world. And the warning proved to be true for many of the first apostles, who were persecuted for their faith, spent time in jail, and many whose lives were martyred. But the lesson applies to modern-day followers in its own way. When Jesus called Peter and Andrew, he didn't promise "follow me, and make sure you get a front-row parking spot." He didn't sell himself with the offer, "follow me, and I'll solve all your financial, relational, and health problems!" No, he said, "Come, follow me . . . and I'll show you how to fish for people" (Matt 4:19). And yet, we pray for these things, and then find ourselves disappointed when God doesn't make them appear. Where did we come up with these expectations of prayer in the first place? How did we so pervert the meaning of faith?

Of course, following Christ does improve our lives. Searching our hearts to discover why we pray naturally leads us to examine why we have chosen the journey of faith in the first place. What does our relationship with Christ offer us? Purpose? Hope? Peace? Redemption? Salvation? Actually, instead of coming to a collective response to that question, I am asking you to discover the answer to that question for yourself, as it is deeply personal.

I expect your response is not "I follow Christ so that I can snag a winning lottery ticket" or "I give my life to Christ so that I won't get cancer." Yet still we expect these things—or more reasonable petitions—and we use prayer as a venue for requesting them. Here, we see the vending machine exchange of goods concept clearly. When we expect God to change our circumstances in exchange for our faithfulness, our prayers are focused mainly on asking for what we want. This can lead to a crisis of faith when a request goes unfulfilled. We might question God's goodness or love, or God's desire for good in our

16

lives. We wonder if God is really real, if God actually cares, or if God is doling out punishment in anger or judgment.

These recurring tensions and questions are always with us, and with the people in our midst. Even if you are a longtime leader of prayer, I urge you to consider regularly re-examining your expectations of prayer for yourself and those whom you lead. As pastors and leaders, we must maintain our own basic understanding and have some answers, in order to guide others.

So, What Does Prayer Do?

After establishing why we have engaged with a life of faith, we find more clarity about why we pray. I hope it is more than a time to ask for what we want out of life. It's not that we should never bring a petition to God. As I outlined above, God cares and wants to know us, and sharing our petitions is one of the many ways we build that relationship. But when we always expect our prayer to manifest a more convenient life, we have gotten a little off track. Santa Claus might be a better outlet for our wish list. There is another way to use prayer, which is less focused on petition and more focused on transformation.

I seek a prayer strategy that focuses on surrendering our own will so that God can transform us. After all, the only thing we have the power to change is ourselves. Paul outlines this transformation in Romans 12:1-2: "So, brothers and sisters, because of God's mercies, I encourage you to present your bodies as a living sacrifice that is holy and pleasing to God. This is your appropriate priestly service. Don't be conformed to the patterns of this world, but be transformed by the renewing of your minds so that you can figure out what God's will is . . ." First, we offer ourselves as sacrifice. That means our desires, hopes, dreams, and wishes are all laid before God. We submit and surrender, acknowledging that God is God, and that we are not God. Second, we open ourselves to the renewing of our minds. This is the rhythm of death and resurrection to new life, which we know well as Christians. It is the central story of our faith, and we are invited to enter into the cycle of new life daily.

Doing so means we come out of prayer changed. What, specifically, needs to change in order for us to live a resurrected life? We begin to pray the prayer

17

of Jesus: "thy will be done." When we do so, our petitions start to sound more like "help me to be faithful, help me to find peace, grant me strength." We become less focused on outcomes and more focused on how to be faithful in the midst of whatever circumstance we find ourselves in. This is the transformation and renewal of our minds that Christ offers.

John 14:13-14 states: "I will do whatever you ask for in my name, so that the Father can be glorified in the Son. When you ask me for anything in my name, I will do it." This, and other similar texts, are some of the most troublesome texts about prayer. It seems to promise that as long as we offer "in Jesus name" at the close of our prayer, we can get just about anything we desire. But perhaps "in my name" means something more like "within my will." Commentator Charles John Ellicot suggests this interpretation of the pericope:

> The prayer of Gethsemane—"If it be possible, let this cup pass from Me: nevertheless, not My will, but Thine be done," should teach what prayer in the name and spirit of Christ means. We commonly attach to our prayers, 'through Jesus Christ our Lord.' We do not always bear in mind that this implies an absolute self-sacrifice, and is a prayer that our very prayers may not be answered except in so far as they are in accordance with the divine will.[3]

My preschool-aged children absolutely adored everything about me today when I gave them maple leaf cookies and apple cider for a snack. They exclaimed, "Mom, you're the best!" and "Mom, I love you so much!" But just a few hours later, when I held them accountable to eating their broccoli at the dinner table, the tide changed quickly. Now they asked, "Mom, why do you hate me?" I fear that my prayer life can sound similar. When I get what I want I'm all praise and thanksgiving, but boy the moment something isn't going so well, I can lament with the best of them. My hope is that the more I pray to be more like God, the more I can tame those temper tantrums.

Oh to have the faith of Shadrach, Meshach, and Abednego! Not only do they have the coolest names ever, the faith they display when they are about to be thrown into a fiery furnace is so unbelievably inspiring! Their courage is unmatched when they stand up to King Nebuchadnezzar himself and declare, "If our God—the one we serve—is able to rescue us from the furnace of flaming fire and from your power, Your Majesty, then let him rescue us. But if he doesn't, know this for certain, Your Majesty: we will never serve your

18

gods or worship the gold statue you've set up" (Dan 3:17-18). "But even if he doesn't . . ." Now that I think of it, perhaps every single petition lifted up to God should be followed by those words. Even if he doesn't . . . I will still praise God. Even if he doesn't . . . I will still worship God.

To foster that kind of faith, I require a transformation of the heart. And so, my prayer work begins. God, make me braver—to face power structures that tempt me to forsake you. God, pour out your sustaining grace when the fiery flames are relentlessly burning all around me. God, surround me with companions on the journey. God, make me faithful to you, even when I am persecuted or treated unfairly. God, help me trust you when I don't understand how the end of the story will work out.

We encourage you to foster and develop your own theology of prayer intentionally, especially concerning what prayer does and does not do. You will lead with greater clarity and integrity, and you'll be able to offer insight and guidance to others as they work out these questions for themselves, too.

CHAPTER TWO

Preparing the Pastoral Prayer

If someone were to ask us how we write our pastoral prayer each week we might well reply, "Seldom the same way." We likely have a general method, though it varies. Hopefully, we get caught up in a mystery, a process much larger than ourselves. We ask for God's grace as we begin.

Getting Started

Finding a place to start is always the challenge. Sometimes a great prayer idea comes early in the week, like a gift of gold! Sometimes a current event dominates the weekly news. Sometimes a dear friend dies, and we find it hard to think about anything else. Sometimes we do not have a clue. Searching for a beginning point is imperative. So, where should we start?

We need to know the sermon's theme to be in-step with the emphasis of the service. Is the sermon part of a series? Does it grow out of the lectionary? Is there a working title? We want to avoid turning our prayer into a mini-message that preempts the sermon.

Having the principal scripture is also essential. Perhaps we read it multiple times in different translations, prayerfully seeking God's heart. Is it from the prophets? Is it wisdom literature? Is it a teaching text? Is it a story with characters? If so, what are their personal, economic, political, and spiritual concerns? It helps to keep a running list on a notepad at our side.

Does the principal scripture have a predominant theological emphasis, like sin and forgiveness? Doubt and faith? Judgment and justice? Healing and hope? Are the sacraments being celebrated? Is a particular ministry of the congregation being recognized?

We should also consider which liturgy or responsive readings are being used. Are there affirmations of faith, unison confessions, or ascriptions of glory? What hymns or praise music have been chosen? Sometimes it helps to sing them while attending to the words that catch our attention, and add them to our list. We can then familiarize ourselves with all the possibilities for these key words and phrases to find their way into the prayer, or to give us a starting point.

Searching for the Right Material

All week long we try to stay tuned to what is going on in the world. We pay attention to local and national news. Hopefully, we are learning from as many perspectives as possible about what people might bring with them into the sanctuary.

We try to imagine what breaks God's heart. Like the boy Samuel, we plead, "Speak, LORD. Your servant is listening" (1 Sam 3:9). We listen to what is being shared with us in crowded hallway conversations, and we listen during that hour of counseling we offered, or at a hospital bedside when a sister or brother pours out their soul. We listen to identify concerns with universal application while carefully honoring each person's privacy.

Has someone just confessed a threatening indiscretion? Did somebody lose their job? Does a cancer sufferer no longer believe in God? Is a long-time member ready to leave the church because we keep ignoring the suffering of people on the edges, or because church politics have become too progressive? What are we hearing, and what is not being said that deserves a voice? This is all prayer material. We take notes. We ask questions, like: What images and metaphors are surfacing? Are we reminded of scenes from movies; songs; or stories from sports, literature, or history?

Listening with Our Heart

Practice and watchfulness are important habits, and so is learning to differentiate our hearts from the hearts of our people. It takes time to develop these, and other habits, as a prayer leader. The potential sources that shape a prayer are limitless, and we can't include everything, every time, in prayer.

Great lines must be cut and, perhaps, saved for another week. (That's why we keep files!) We must weed out the unnecessary.

We would be wise to **read the Psalms** regularly, Psalms being the great prayer book of our spiritual ancestors. For good reason Jesus memorized them. We can imagine, for instance, how we might work the opening verses of Psalm 139 into our prayer: "O gracious Lord, You have searched us thoroughly. You understand us better than we'll ever understand ourselves. You know our thoughts, our ambitions, our worries and fears."

Or, we could do something similar with Psalm 51: "Have mercy upon us, O God. As we open our hearts before You receive our confessions. Wash us. Cleanse us from our sin. Forgive us when we miss the mark." Why not borrow thoughts from some of the greatest prayers ever written, paraphrasing them into our own words, words God can use and people can grasp?

It is tremendously helpful to **keep a prayer journal**. Criteria for entry might include things that move you to tears of sadness or joy. If you gain a new self-awareness, write it down. If God surprises you with an experience that you've never had, that goes in too. Sometimes a word is given to you, a phrase or a sentence. Try always to secure your journal entries with a scripture reference that keeps you humble and anchored to your tradition. We are not the first to walk these valleys and plateaus.

Making It Interesting and Accessible

You must wrestle to find the best verbs and adjectives. Strive to keep sentences short. Long sentences lose people. A seminary professor once admonished our class: "Cut your sentences until they bleed!" Streamline your thoughts, focus on the essential points. We recommend using common language. And we urge you to avoid imposing theological terms.

Above all, we don't want the prayer to draw attention to ourselves. We don't want to come off as dramatic performers. We don't want to be divisive. Instead, we pray to be invisible. We're not addressing the congregation as we pray, but rather we're speaking directly to God! We are there, serving on behalf of people as their priests. Our desire is to listen carefully enough during the week to carry their fears and hopes and joys to the throne of God.

Navigating Tricky Holidays

Offering a pastoral prayer to commemorate a holiday is a task filled with potential landmines.

Take Mother's Day, for instance. Some worshippers are grieving the loss of their mothers. Some have strained relationships. Some are longing for a positive pregnancy test. There are mothers who have lost children. Interpersonal relationships and family dynamics are under a spotlight. Many other worshippers may be filled with sentimentality, appreciation, and tenderness in thanking God for their family. What a task to know how to lead a prayer that blesses all and alienates none! Acknowledging that the room holds a variety of experiences and feelings, and that God is both a safe refuge and a leading guide for each person, is key. Show the same sensitivity on Father's Day as well.

Holidays such as the Fourth of July, Memorial Day, and Veterans Day present an opportunity to thank God for our country, freedom, and the sacrifices of those who have served in the military. Try to find a balance between celebrating the goodness of living in America while also praying for God's continued guidance for our country as we repent from systemic racism and other ways our nation has missed the mark. Although it started as a holiday to honor those who have given their lives in service to their country, over time Memorial Day has expanded to be a time to visit graves and remember any loved ones who have gone before us. Recognize both layers in your pastoral prayer.

It is hard to not let political agendas drive. Try to aim for light touches rather than deep dives on each of these different dynamics. Help all congregants know their experience is recognized.

Most importantly, always bring your prayer back to Jesus and his power to redeem, restore, heal, renew, and love the brokenness of our world.

Getting Un-Stuck

Some weeks during the composition process, especially when I'm stuck, I (Steve) offer a prayer something like this:

Jesus, help me take the words I've been hearing all week long and as I stand before the altar table, lift them up on behalf of the ones who spoke them. May they prove sincere offerings to You who first gave them. And may Your beloved daughters and sons hear a word from You in response. Please, Holy Spirit, take it from here.

Take comfort in remembering that we never craft our prayers alone. We have one who intercedes on our behalf with deep sighs and unexpressed groans (Rom 8:26-27). When a precise word is essential, it will be provided. If not, it wasn't essential.

Making It Participatory

Invite the congregation's participation in your prayers. Build in pauses for silent prayer. Begin with active and engaging words of praise and adoration, glorifying God. Use phrases from opening hymns or praise music that are fresh in people's ears.

Then move to thanksgiving. Share a few specific examples of gratitude that you've gathered during the week, then say, "Hear now our silent prayers of thanksgiving." Pause for ten seconds or longer. You should pray silently yourself, too, leaving plenty of time for people to think of their own reasons for gratitude and ways to express it.

We suggest that you continue with some form of confession, relying heavily on notes from pastoral conversations and current events. Review your prayer journal for insights gained about your own inadequacies and failures. Remember what the Lord requires: to do justice, to love kindness, and to walk humbly with our God (Mic 6:8). Reflect, also, on your own failure to do these things. Write out several examples. Then you might say, "Hear now our silent prayers of confession." Make space for another pause, again allowing plenty of time for people really to experience repentance.

This is followed with prayers of petition. Here, you should remember the needs you've encountered in the previous week or days. Remember where you've been, what you've seen, and where you haven't been but should have gone. Remember forgotten people, people you're uncomfortable with, strangers, and those who don't have anyone to pray for them. Again, allow time for silent prayer for those in need. And again, allow enough time for the people to offer their own prayers.

Finally, as you prepare, save space for two or three sentences to set up the Lord's Prayer. Return the people's attention to God's greatness and grace. Ask God to use you and those who are gathered to work for justice, to build bridges, and to bring hope to our world. We end with Jesus, who is our beginning, end, and in-between; Jesus, "who suffered, died and rose again that we might live and love through him, and who still teaches us to pray together . . ."

Using Inclusive Language

We want to be as inclusive as possible when we lead others in prayer. Our words should be all-encompassing, embracing everybody. Each person should feel our prayers are *for them*, that in God's eyes all are equally loved and celebrated.

Gender neutral expressions are most helpful. We use phrases like humankind, women and men, humanity, all. We are careful and judicious in our use of male terms for God. We use terms like Holy God, Creator, Christ, Holy Spirit, Redeemer, Sustainer, Rock. When we do refer to God as Father, we also find ways to address God as Mother, Father/Mother God, or Holy Parent. This helps us avoid perpetuating the belief that maleness is superior and the norm. (The Lord's Prayer is an exception.) Instead of "His love," we say, "God's love." Instead of "Himself" we say "Godself."

This may feel awkward at first. It takes discipline for us to expand our understanding of who God is. But after a time, it becomes natural, second nature. And it is urgently important to make sure everyone feels welcome in God's sight. Surely God's nature is as completely female as it is male.

Avoiding "I" Language

As leaders lifting prayers for other people, it is important to remember we are praying for *them*, not just for ourselves. Our prayers are not about us, though we are deeply engaged and feel the prayers in a most personal way. We rarely use the words *I* or mine or *my*. Instead, our language should center on the praises and petitions of the community. Jesus taught us to pray using the plural *our* Father, give us *our* daily bread, forgive us *our* trespasses.

Practicing Out Loud

When you're satisfied that you have a prayer to offer on people's behalf, practice it aloud. Listen to the inflection of your voice. You want to calm others, not agitate them. Listen for where you need to slow down or pause so others can catch up. Remind yourself you are not in a race. You also don't want to put people to sleep! Enunciate as clearly as you can and speak loudly enough for those sitting at the back and those wearing hearing devices. Practice, and practice right up to the beginning of worship. Then let it go. Give it to God to infuse with spirit and truth. It is so true that to prepare the pastoral prayer is to get caught up in an immense mystery, in wonders beyond our comprehension.

Giving Due Credit

Occasionally, following worship, someone will express appreciation for the prayer. When this happens, we urge you to smile and quietly thank them. For an instant, allow yourself to bask in the glow of satisfaction. Reflect on how the whole prayer process has fed you. Think of Jesus saying to his disciples, "'I have food to eat that you do not know about'" (John 4:32). Writing a prayer nourishes us. Let us be proud of God, who never quits or gives up, nor does he ever stop believing in us, equipping us, or anointing us with divine power to craft and speak on God's behalf.

We are proud of God, who wants and wills more than anything to be one with us, so that we may be one with each other and one with God (John 17:11). What wondrous love is this, O my soul? What love divine, all loves excelling? What amazing grace. And the most amazing of all is that we get to be part of it!

Thank You, O God, for being who You are and loving us the way You do. Make us, as those who lead others in prayer, worthy not only to pray to You, but for Your daughters and sons. Thank You for making us pray-ers. Keep speaking to us, and we'll do our best to keep listening. Give us Your words, so that Your Word may become flesh, full of grace and truth, living among us and through us, accomplishing abundantly far more than all we can ask or imagine, to the glory, honor, and praise of Jesus Christ. Thank You, God! Thank You, thank You! Amen.

CHAPTER THREE
Delivering the Prayer

Spontaneous Prayer

We've spent a lot of this book discussing preparation for praying, even up to detailed, deliberate word choices. We've discussed rehearsing a prayer prior to praying it in front of a group. Depending on your worship-planning process, you may even need to have something prepared ahead of time for the team you work with. Preparation, forethought, and deliberate planning help us honor our role as the prayer leader. But what about spontaneous prayer? For some people and some traditions, it feels completely ridiculous to pre-write a prayer. In that case, prayer is Spirit-led; it is organic. It is nothing if it isn't extemporaneous.

Regardless of your personal preference when given a choice, pastors will undoubtedly have moments when they are called upon to pray with no advance notice. Don't panic. When I (Anne) am feeling ill-prepared, I remind myself prayer is simply talking to God. In these situations, it is more like talking to God with a whole bunch of people eavesdropping on my conversation, but I try to forget anyone else is in the room. Other reminders I give myself while I take my time walking up to the microphone include:

1. it doesn't have to be long;

2. it doesn't have to be fancy;

3. I have permission to pause and collect my thoughts throughout the prayer; and

4. I may say aloud what I'm thinking.

29

I really use the prayer to acknowledge the surroundings that I'm observing. For instance, I never like to be standing between a large group of people and a steamy buffet of delicious food. And yet, that's precisely where I stand, at wedding after wedding, being summoned by the DJ to stand in front of a hungry crowd to offer grace over the meal. You better get to the point, Rev. Those folks have had a couple cocktails and they are ready for a plate of chicken marsala. So, what would it hurt simply to name it? I begin my prayer: *"Lord God, we are eager to celebrate this new marriage with food, drink, cake, and dancing but we pause for a moment to acknowledge you . . ."*

Perhaps you find yourself in a contentious committee meeting that needs a reset. This isn't a prayer that you've planned on needing to pray. Still, you feel the Spirit urging you to lead the group to stop and pray. Yes, it's a little intimidating to look that fear in the face and suggest a moment of spiritual intervention, especially if you have no idea what you are going to pray. Start with what you feel in the room:

> *God, you are the Prince of Peace, and yet we feel so far from a peaceful resolution in this room . . .*

Maybe you're out to lunch with a friend whose phone rings and she receives bad news on the other end. You offer to pray:

> *God, we are in shock. We weren't expecting this. We can barely form words after hearing such terrible news . . .*

We encourage you simply to start where you are. It is OK to admit within the content of a prayer that sometimes it is hard to know what to pray. Likely, whatever you are feeling is relatable. But even if your prayer isn't what another person in the room would've said, at the very least you're expressing genuine, heartfelt conversation to God, which can never be wrong. It is not only faithful, but it also inspires others to offer honest prayer as well.

Transitions to Prayer

Think about how your prayer fits into the flow of your worship service. Even if your congregants know it is coming because the order of service is predictable, or because it's written on a bulletin before them, it is a hospitable gesture to spend just a brief moment explaining what is about to happen next.

There are a few things you can do with this transition time. Introduce yourself if it is the first time you've spoken in the service. Explain what we do in prayer. Answer questions, such as, "Why do we pray?" and "What do we hope to accomplish?" You might acknowledge what can be difficult about prayer or something that might keep the prayer time from being "successful." For instance, you could name the reality that our minds wander and we tend to get distracted. You could acknowledge that sometimes we are mad at God or that sometimes we perceive that God is far away, which can make engaging in prayer more difficult. You might be speaking to people in the seats who are so exhausted they have only just barely made it to the worship service and for whom offering anything more than their sheer presence is too much. How can you make it welcoming? How can you invite people in?

If you are leading into prayer from a powerful offering of song, you might take a moment to thank the choir. You might focus for just a moment on a word that spoke to you from that music, and to connect it to the practice prayer:

> *Great is thy faithfulness . . . what an important reminder that we can trust that God is faithful even when we are tired and weary! Now we begin a time of prayer where we put our lives in the hands of that trustworthy guide, our Lord.*

You might tell a very brief story of something that happened to you this week that helps folks see God in a new way. These brief stories can also help you connect or gain authority with your community:

> *This week I had the windows in my home washed. It was the first time in the five years we lived there that they have been washed and I was amazed at how much brighter my home is! I could see everything a little more clearly. It reminded me of something Jesus said, in Matthew chapter thirteen, verse thirteen, when he challenges His listeners: "This is why I speak to the crowds in parables: although they see, they don't really see; and although they hear, they don't really hear or understand." We take time to be transformed in prayer so that we might grow into followers who can truly see and under-stand the message of Jesus.*

> *My kids, ages six and three, have started playing hide and seek in the back of the car. While I'm driving. While they are strapped into their seatbelt and car seat. They have nowhere to go, no way to hide themselves, but still they*

count to ten and seek one another—they shriek in delight when they are found! It reminds me of Psalm 139 and God's promise that there is no place we can go to hide from God. I remind you, as we enter a time of prayer, that we can never run from this God who loves us endlessly.

Take care you don't preach the sermon before the sermon. But a concise, well-thought-out story or connection to a theological thought can help ready our hearts for prayer. You wouldn't have time for each of these options every time, of course. Vary it from week to week if you are praying before the same crowd. Whatever you choose, or however you vary your introductions, a couple sentences of set-up make a big difference.

Regardless of how you set a theological framework, it is also helpful to give a word of instruction. In my first years of ministry, I (Anne) was taught to explain what you are doing before you do every piece of a service. If your community is focused on welcoming guests and inviting folks to church who are less familiar with religious practices, a word of instruction helps people feel more comfortable engaging if they either have never done it before or have not for many years. Nothing is worse than sitting in the pew of an unfamiliar church and not knowing when to stand, kneel, or sit; what page to look for; or what to say when. Assume you always have someone new in your midst. Even if you don't, giving clear instructions will remind your community to begin inviting their neighbors and friends; it will give them confidence that if they do, their friend will feel comfortable their first time attending. Below is an example of setting a theological framework:

I'm going to lead us through this prayer and then there will be a time to offer your own personal prayers to God in silence and I'll let you know when we have come to that portion. At the end, we will close by praying the Lord's Prayer together. The words will be on the screen (or in the bulletin), if you'd like to pray them aloud with us. Would you join me now in prayer?

If you are invited to lead a prayer at a commencement celebration or a luncheon for the local Rotary Club, a brief word of transition will be helpful in that setting as well. How will you invite engagement from those who hear the word *Pastor* in your introduction and are tempted automatically to check out? How will you show generosity toward those who ascribe to a different faith tradition? A concise and compelling set-up will grab attention and gain trust quickly.

Posture

As you consider the delivery of your prayer, posture is important. Our bodies communicate the message behind the prayer as much as the words themselves do. Your worship space may allow for kneeling, which for many people is the most prayerful stance. But circumstances such as physical ability, furniture availability, or other considerations may not allow for kneeling.

I (Anne) can still see in my mind's eye, at my childhood church, how my pastor would walk through the aisles collecting names to pray for and then settle at the front of the congregation at the bottom step leading up to the chancel. There he would bow his body so low it seemed he was trying to lower himself so deeply into the ground as to disappear entirely. There must have been days when his knees hurt, or his back was uncomfortable. I wonder if he ever felt awkward—the senior leader of our community prostrate on the floor in front of us. But his posture was a priority. It was a commitment he made, a commentary on why and to whom we pray. There was not a doubt in the mind of one single individual in the room what his body language was communicating: full surrender to our God.

If you can place a kneeler on the chancel under the cross, congregants make the connection that you carry their concerns to the cross and humbly lay them before our Lord. Your shoulders are the freeway for the burdens of your community. Your offering creates a passageway through which heavy concerns are laid down and healing, hope, and restoration flow back in return.

If you choose to stand before the community rather than kneel, you may find that opening your hands and arms can express the sentiment that God's love flows through you as a vessel. Your open hands indicate that you are not only offering up the concerns of your people but also that you are open in anticipation to receiving whatever gifts God is about to pour out. From time to time, invite the congregation to mirror that same pose, their hands laid—palms up—on their laps as they begin prayer time.

Aim for a posture that is somehow both relaxed and respectful. Being stiff communicates a rigidity we need less of in the religious world, and yet we do want to honor the prayer time and the One to whom we pray. Our willingness to err on the relaxed side comes from a deep belief that God does not need us to be uncomfortable or stifled in order for God to feel honored.

Admittedly, some of this is personal taste. I am the kind of person who always prefers casual, comfortable clothing. God knows this about me. To put on a suddenly highly formal performance would not make sense unless you regularly wear a clergy robe, which does not automatically dictate stiffness. Perhaps you are a more formal, proper person, in which case a more relaxed pose will not feel right at all. Be true to yourself. Your authentic devotion means more to God than anything else.

Handling Written Prayers

If you choose to offer your prayer by reading a pre-written prayer, consider how your materials are carried. We suggest laying a single sheet of paper on top of (not inside) a flat, black notebook. Minimize opening of notebooks, flipping pages, unfolding papers, or any fumbling with papers that you can. While reading a prayer can be appropriate, memorizing or internalizing your script for the introduction and transition to prayer will feel more natural.

Underscoring a Prayer

If you've never experienced a prayer with an underscore, imagine that your life is a movie and there is a poignant soundtrack playing behind you. For many, this instrumental music that plays quietly in the background while the prayer is delivered improves the entire experience. From a selfish viewpoint, I (Anne) don't feel so much pressure to fill in the silence of the room. I feel more freedom to take my time, allow pauses, and know there will be something pleasant to listen to filling in the gaps of my actual words.

From a worship-planning point of view, underscoring throughout certain portions of the service can help tie the pieces together to the whole. Musicians can make a seamless flow between songs of praise into instrumental music that serves as a backdrop to the prayer. Perhaps you stay on the chords from the previous song or move into the chords of the song that is to come. But either way, this music greatly improves the ambience of the worship space during prayer.

Praying in a Room of People with Closed Eyes

It is an odd thing to stand in front of a room of people whose eyes are supposedly closed. Assume someone is watching. Absolutely refrain from using a prayer moment to adjust an undergarment or wipe your nose.

You, as the leader, should also have your eyes cast down, either fully shut, gazing at the floor, or reading your prayer text. Having your eyes shut can have a dizzying affect, so there may be times when you need your eyes to remain open. We hope you don't have this same problem because it causes all kinds of awkward squirming when your stare accidentally meets another person's stare during the middle of a prayer. It is better to focus on the toe of your shoe or your written prayer text.

Allowing a Time of Silent Prayer

Often, a pastoral prayer will include a time of silence for one purpose or another (Steve wrote about this in a previous section). Always lead the congregation into that time of silence with clear instructions about how it is to be used. There is nothing worse than a participant being launched into a time of silent prayer without *knowing* that's what's going on. They might think, did I abruptly go deaf? Is the speaker having a medical emergency? What is going on? Then they may look around the room for a sign of what is going on. You must always, always let folks know to expect a time of silent prayer. We recommend you use the phrase *silent prayer* rather than *silence* if your prayers are underscored with instrumental music, which makes it not a truly silent time. You might also use the word *pause*, which works with or without a musical underscore. Conversely, if you offer instructions about what might be prayed, without ever explicitly saying that those prayers are to be offered silently, guests might assume they are being invited to speak their prayers aloud.

Silent prayer in public is a rather mysterious thing, especially for the nonreligious, or those who are new to church. To make the most hospitable environment, these instructions help folks know what to expect and how to engage, avoiding confusion or anxiety. Additionally, it is helpful to be specific when you introduce the time of silent prayer. What, specifically, do you suggest that a person should pray during this time of silence?

Rather than simply saying "God hear us in this time of silent prayer," transition to silence by suggesting that the congregation "share with God the burdens that weigh heavy on you this morning," or "as you review the past week, confess your shortcomings—those ways you fallen short of God's call for your life." The more concrete and specific your lead-in instructions are, the more likely participants will be to engage in that time with God.

The goal is to leave enough time, but not too much time, for silent prayer. The pastor is left with a few different options. First, she or he can use the silent prayer to offer her or his own silent prayers. When the pastor has completed her or his own silent prayers, the pastor can transition back into the remainder of the prayer.

Allowing for that silence can be one of the most difficult parts of delivering a prayer. Years ago, I (Anne) led the pastoral prayer, said "Amen," and then returned to my seat next to the pastor I was serving with. He leaned over and gently suggested, "I can tell you weren't praying during the silent prayer time because you didn't leave enough time." I thought to myself, *if I left enough time for all my confessions, we would be here all day!*

Another option is to count to thirty, or another designated amount of time, and move forward with the prayer after the allotted amount of time. I have found this works better for me. It keeps me focused on something so my mind doesn't wander. I am more confident that I have left a reasonable amount of time for silent prayer, and I commit to offering my own silent prayers to God in a different setting.

Prayer Voice

Don't alter your normal speaking voice to speak to God. If you are a preacher, perhaps you have what is called a "preaching voice." We invite you to ask folks who have listened to offer you some honest feedback about that. It is startling, and a little off-putting, to hear someone's voice change simply because they began speaking in front of a crowd. It can seem insincere. People might give you the benefit of the doubt, assuming the change in vocal quality is due to your respect for the role of praying. Perhaps, for some, a voice change enables a Spirit-filled mindset in communicating. But, in general, we find that people are yearning for authenticity in their leaders, and it rings false or showy to change one's voice for leading prayer. We encourage you to gather feedback and prayerfully discern whether a performing voice is helpful in communicating your message.

Some situations, particular worship themes, or specific praise songs will fire you up, and you may just run with it, letting the Spirit be on the loose. Your phrasing might be more dramatic, your volume more dynamic, or the pace more roller-coastery. This voice communicates prophetic challenge as opposed to pastoral shepherding, which may be more common in many contexts. Sometimes you'll walk away thinking, "I missed the mark today." Try something a little different next time. Be intentional with the tools you have: tone, inflection, pacing, and articulation all matter. If you think as carefully about them as you would the themes, words, and flow of your prayer, then your presentation style will appropriately match the prayer you have composed.

Prayer Duration

How long should a prayer be? We sure hope there is no right answer! We trust that God knows that the length doesn't indicate anything about the heart behind the prayer. Sometimes all we have the gumption for is one word, as Anne Lamott expresses in her book *Help, Thanks, Wow.* These are often the most heartfelt, bravest prayers we can pray.

Even the most compelling prayer can be difficult to engage with after a period of time. The people you lead in prayer are in a passive role. They're not coming up with the words but are simply listening and trying to engage with yours. How long is the human attention span? In 2015, *Time* reported[1] that the human attention span had decreased from twelve seconds to eight seconds. Critics of our fast-paced, "just Google it," Amazon Prime one-day-delivery world were quick to point out that even the notoriously distractable goldfish has a nine-second attention span, which is now longer than humans'. Our hope is that the time shared in holy prayer is an exception, but we all think our thing is the exception. I (Anne) aim for a pastoral prayer around three and a half minutes, including the Lord's Prayer, which accounts for a little more than thirty seconds.

When my prayer is too long it is because I am trying to do too much. I may be trying to cover too many topics, teach more than I should, or find answers that aren't there. Usually, less is more. I do better when I lean into the mystery and power of Almighty God.

One Sunday, I felt the tempo of the underscore increasing ever so slightly over the course of my prayer. I asked the worship leader about it later, wondering if it was my imagination or if it were real. Apparently, I was getting a little long-winded and he confessed he can affect the tempo of my prayer by adjusting his underscore. We would all be so lucky to have such helpful colleagues. Mostly, we laugh about it. But, honestly, it is powerful to know that someone standing behind you has your back and will urge you forward when you need it.

Interruptions

The number of interruptions that can occur while leading a public prayer is absolutely infinite. Where there are people gathered, the possibilities are endless. Where there is technology involved, Lord help us. Any prayer that *isn't* interrupted by a squealing microphone or a screaming child is honestly miraculous. If you do this work long enough, you will definitely have a baby grab your hair and pull (hard!) while you are praying over her baptismal water. There will be a man who is strung out on drugs in the front row calling out "Alleluia!" at all the wrong times.

Almost always, we recommend ignoring whatever you hear and moving forward unflinchingly. Without wavering, dig into your focus and continue on. No matter how curious you are, no matter how funny the noise is, be unwavering. In fact, plan on being interrupted. Plan for something to go wrong so that when it does, you can nod knowingly and move forward.

On rare occasions, you may need to pause to acknowledge the distraction. Only in the case that it is so dramatic, so persistent, that literally every person in the room hears it. And then, only pause if you can easily find a way to acknowledge it *in a way that will feel pastoral and helpful*. If you can think of nothing creative to say that would feel prayerful and grace-filled, just ignore the distraction. Don't try to be funny or clever. Be prayerful.

Thunderstorms, though. We live and serve in the Midwest where thunderstorms are common, especially throughout late spring and summer. If there is a boom of thunder while I (Anne) am praying, of course it's just too tempting not to thank God: "We hear you, thank you for joining us, for reminding us you are there." The other easy connecting point is in the case of sirens. The sound of an emergency vehicle might automatically elicit a prayerful response. When you know a police car, ambulance, or fire truck is barreling by your worship service, it is so simple to pause and request protection for those who are in need of help, and offer a prayer of gratitude for those who serve.

When babies are crying, a band member knocks over a guitar as they are trying to exit the chancel, or a friend with Tourette's is having a triggering moment, your congregation will appreciate an unflappable leader, marching forward without missing a beat. Trust whichever staff and volunteers are in the room to take care of an emergency or offer hospitality if it is needed. The prayer goes on.

Praying in Smaller Settings

In more intimate settings, adjust your prayer delivery to a more personal feel. If you are leading the prayer at the conclusion of a small group, take time to include prayer requests that were shared during the session. Use verbiage that was shared, repeat phrases that you heard, and really show that you were listening throughout your time together.

In small collections of people, it can be meaningful if each member is prayed for by name. Please don't make the same mistake as me (Anne). One of my worst prayer mistakes was diving in to pray for each person by name, when I realized my mind was completely blank on one person's name. I can still feel the pit in my stomach. I knew it started with a "J." *Jason? Jeremy? Josh? None of those is right.* After stalling for a moment, I turned to him, opened my eyes, and asked, "What's your name, again?" It was terribly embarrassing, and I can barely believe I am admitting to it now, except I hope that my sharing will, first, remind you that we are all going to mess up from time to time; and, second, save you from this particular mistake in your own prayer ministry.

Intimate, personal moments in prayer can be so meaningful when they are done well. Take a risk, write down notes of important information and names, if you need to, and get personal!

Part Two

THE PRAYERS

CHAPTER FOUR

How We Choose Our Words

When we lead prayer, we must choose our words carefully. It is a holy task. Guiding people in prayer, we function both as pastor and as priest, by lifting prayers to God on our congregation's behalf. Ancient priests received gifts of livestock and grain from their people, and then the priests would burn the gifts on the altar as worship offerings. We continue this practice by reverently lifting words from our people's hearts to give praise, make confession, and submit petition: "Lord, hear our prayers."

Recently I (Steve) coached a fledgling pastor in his prayer preparation. He submitted his previous weekend's prayer, and we went over it line-by-line. He felt good about what he had written but asked for suggestions as to how he might improve. I showed him some of my prayers, not to suggest they were better, but to demonstrate my word selection process. For the next several weeks we continued this practice. First, we discussed what he liked best in his prayer, and then we considered what he might say differently and what he might delete. After several weeks of practice, he no longer needed a mentor.

What follows are examples of my recent pastoral prayers; they are humble offerings, lifted reverently to God. I will pretend you, the reader, are at my side. I pray that my comments instruct and do not confuse. One of my teachers used to quip, "Just because the water is muddy doesn't mean it is deep!"

Transition to Prayer #1

Hi, my name is Steve Langhofer. I am one of the pastors here at Resurrection. I am coming to believe something firmly about prayer: that God yearns for these quiet moments with us even more than we do. And

I am coming to believe something else: that during prayer, God speaks to those who listen. Let's pray.

Comment: It is important always to introduce ourselves. We never know who is in the congregation for the first time. Each week I also try to share one idea as part of my invitation to pray, something to prime people's spiritual pump, to start them thinking about why we pray.

Pastoral and Lord's Prayers #1

O loving and listening God, we worship You. We thank You for guiding us as we journey. Thank You for quenching our thirst and satisfying our hunger. For calming our anxious fears. For shining upon us with redeeming grace. For leading us in right paths. So many times this week You've been there for us. Hear our silent prayers of praise and thanksgiving. (Pause.)

Comment: I prefer to begin by expressing thanks. It seems a good and right thing to do. In the first phrase, I not only acknowledged that God is love but also that God is a listener, which I hinted at in my transition (Ex 3:7). By the end of the first sentence, I made clear that praying is our worship. We start with God, not with ourselves: "We worship You." I capitalize You, lest I forget who I am addressing and into Whose holy Presence I come. Then I begin detailing why: because of God's guidance, God's quenching and satisfying, and God's calming, shining, and redeeming presence. These are lots of active verbs. God is a Doer! Where do I get my verbs? Often from the opening hymns we just sang.

Then we pause for at least ten seconds. This is not just my prayer. This prayer is also coming from the people. Hopefully, my opening verbiage has touched something positive in their past week for which they can give thanks.

We confess our difficulty in getting along with each other. We think to ourselves, "Why can't everybody have the same opinion as me?" We become irritable, rude, prone to seek our own advantage. We are quick to condemn others, and sometimes ourselves. We do not listen well. Lord, in Your mercy, hear our silent confessions. (Pause.)

Comment: Now I am setting us up for silent confession. I want to stimulate people's thinking, to make our sin specific while remaining general enough that everybody can acknowledge a need to say, "I'm sorry, Lord." We do not get along with each other. We think it is all about us. We have a bad attitude. We do not listen. Remember that I suggested listening in the opening transition? By now most of us have realized a need to make confession. (FYI . . . this had been a contentious week in Congress between Democrats and Republicans. I knew it was on everyone's heart. I felt I needed to help our people pray about it. This time I chose not to name it outright. Sometimes I do.) Again, we pause long enough for individual prayer.

Lord, show us what saddens Your heart. Help us see as You see. When we are in pain, or confused, or sad, or angry, or feeling defensive, it is hard for us to hear You. Teach us about ourselves in these stressful moments. Teach us how to love as You love. Teach us when we need to lighten up on our judgments against each other and against ourselves.

Comment: Here's a shift to imagine things from God's perspective. Can we imagine what saddens God's heart, and what it is like to see as God sees (1 Cor 13:4-7)? Surely it saddens God when we do not listen well. Surely it gladdens God's heart when we avail ourselves to be taught. Notice we have moved from confession into petition, making requests of God, seeking God's help.

We pray for victims of domestic terrorism, most recently in our religious communities of New York and Texas. For those dealing with fires in Australia. For those grieving great losses. For those who need healing in body, mind, and spirit. For those homeless, and country-less, for whom there is no room in the inn. For those who feel they are not important and don't matter. Hear our prayers for those in need. (Pause.)

Comment: Go full speed ahead into petition and supplication! We get very specific; we might reference headlines from the week's news. We lay these things on the altar before God: terrorism, fire, grief, illness, and those without a place to live. Then we make another significant pause to let it all sink in and to add our private requests.

Thank You for treasuring these moments of prayer. So do we. We pray in the name of Jesus who still teaches us to pray together, "Our Father, who art in heaven, hallowed be Thy name. Thy kingdom come, Thy will

45

be done on earth as it is in heaven. Give us this day our daily bread. And forgive us our trespasses as we forgive those who trespass against us. And lead us—not into temptation, but deliver us from evil. For Thine is the kingdom, and the power, and the glory forever. Amen."

Comment: We wrap everything together with more thanksgiving. We cannot thank God too much, especially for the intimacy of prayer. And we go back to the opening transition's emphasis on prayer as listening, God's and ours. I like to lead into the Lord's Prayer each week remembering Jesus is risen from the dead, by saying the words, "Jesus who still teaches us to pray together," even as he did the first time. This is what gives us hope more than anything.

Transition to Prayer #2

Hi, my name is Steve Langhofer. I'm one of the pastors here at Resurrection. I call us to prayer, knowing that the God who made us loves us and celebrates us every day.

Comment: This call to prayer is brief. I wanted to save most of my limited prayer time for the pastoral prayer. I did, however, take time to set a positive reminder that God loves and celebrates us. This is all the more reason to approach God with the reassurance that God is for us, not against us.

Pastoral and Lord's Prayers #2

O Creator God, from whom all blessings come, we praise You! For the beauty of Your earth and the glory of Your skies, we raise our grateful praise. You are good. You are just. You are overflowing with compassion. You make us resilient. You never let us down. You make it well with our souls. Thank You.

Comment: Our theme for the day was God's good creation. Our opening hymns named it, so I carried that into my beginning sentences. I reflected our doxology of praise: God's beauty, justice, compassion, and God's steadfast seeking our well-being. We have much for which to be thankful.

Lord, we often disappoint ourselves. We worry too much about our mistakes. We are our own worst critics. But You pronounce us good even though some days we find that hard to believe. Hear now our silent prayers of confession. (Pause.)

Comment: Despite God's goodness surrounding us, we focus on the negative. Often, we don't like ourselves and fixate on our failure. Yet God's unbelievable grace enables us to approach God without fear and to honestly confess our resistance to God's love. We need a moment of silence to think about that. I try to use simple language that everyone can understand by minimizing religious jargon.

Heal us, Lord. Set us right with You. Help us trust You in all things. To not lose heart. To not be afraid. To live and work justly, practicing kindness and walking humbly. To be instruments of peace, sowing love, light, and joy. To bear witness to Your grace and power. Fill us with Your Holy Spirit. Make us strong in faith.

Comment: This paragraph is a form of absolution. God forgives our sin by healing us, setting things right between us, teaching us to trust, and having hope instead of fear. God's forgiveness frees us to work for justice, to practice kindness and humility (Mic 6). It also frees us to exercise Saint Francis's virtues of peace and light, love and joy, thereby gracefully bearing witness to God's power through the Holy Spirit.

We pray for those who are victims of shootings, for those who shoot them, and for the rest of us who believe something different has got to be done to stop the killings. We remember the seventy-fifth anniversary tomorrow of the liberation of the concentration camp at Auschwitz, Poland. We pray for the earth, our life partner. You love it; help us love it and to act accordingly. We pray for our Congress, for Representatives and Senators who are trying hard to be faithful to the best interests of our country. Bless and guide them. We pray for those who are hospitalized, those who have lost loved ones, those in recovery from addiction. We pray for each other, and for all, anywhere, who are in need. Hear our silent prayers. (Pause.)

Comment: This was a heavy news week. There were horrific shootings and a Holocaust anniversary. I also brought back our creation theme alongside the need for creative solutions to conflict among national leaders. Every week I try to include prayers for the sick and grieving, and those in prison or addiction recovery. We almost couldn't pause too long in silence for all this.

We pray this in the name of Jesus who brings and holds all things together, in heaven and on Your good earth, and who still teaches us to pray together, "Our Father, who art in heaven, hallowed be Thy name. Thy kingdom come, Thy will be done on earth as it is in heaven. Give us this day our daily bread. And forgive us our trespasses as we forgive those who trespass against us. And lead us—not into temptation, but deliver us from evil. For Thine is the kingdom, and the power, and the glory forever. Amen."

Comment: I always want to bring us back to Jesus, who labors on our behalf in this good earth and in the next, still teaching us to pray together. I like to work in short passages of scripture, such as Colossians 1:17, priming us for his sanctifying prayer.

Transition to Prayer #3

Hi, my name is Steve Langhofer. I'm one of the pastors here at Resurrection. What we do next is surely one of God's favorite parts of our worship, when we open our hearts and lift our prayers. This is true. Let's pray.

Comment: I love calls to prayer that are short and to the point, a simple reminder that God loves and waits patiently to hear from us. As Kierkegaard instructs, in worship, God is the audience, and we are the actors.

Pastoral and Lord's Prayers #3

O God, we worship You. We praise You with our whole being as long as we live! We praise You for the beauty of Your creation. For Your faithfulness. For giving justice to the oppressed and sight to the blind, and for straightening those who are bent low. For Your strength. For Your protection. We praise You!

Comment: The first sentence reminds us what we are gathered to do: to worship with our whole being, with all that is in us, the One who gives us life (Ps 103:1); to worship God's beauty in creation; to worship God's faithfulness; to worship God's justice, healing, strength, and protection. All these images came from our opening hymns today.

Thank You for revealing Yourself in Jesus. When we lose our direction, we get reoriented to him. When we forget our purpose, we find it again in him. When we get fuzzy about who we are, we rediscover ourselves in him. When we feel distant from You, he's the one who reminds us that You are as close as our breathing, and You love us too much to leave us alone.

Comment: Here we begin by giving thanks for God's self-revelation in Jesus. Jesus is the center of our lives. He's the one who, through his living spirit, is our unquenchable light in the darkness (John 1:5). We are good to give him our full attention when leading our people in prayer.

Keep us sensitive like him. Forgive us when we cause hurt. Help us know when to reach out and when to back off. We never know what prior hurtful experiences each other carries. Help us learn from our mistakes. Give us courage to apologize. Make us humble enough to receive apologies. Grant us mercy always and hold us in Your grace. Hear our silent prayers. (Pause.)

Comment: This paragraph was dedicated to the numerous people I spoke with this week struggling in relationships, people who were struggling to understand and forgive others. They were also struggling to honor the boundaries of others and themselves, and struggling to say "Sorry," and to receive the apology of another. I'm lifting up real people's prayers here without identifying them. I could literally visualize particular individuals on their knees in silent confession: "God, show mercy to me, a sinner" (Luke 18:13).

We pray for those who are sick, and those in pain. We pray for those who need a good cry. And those who do not forgive themselves. For those who cannot sleep. For those troubled about death. For those who need a friend. For those learning that You specialize in healing broken hearts. Hear our silent prayers. (Pause.)

Comment: This paragraph spills over from the one above. There are different levels of sickness and pain. There is anguish of the soul and sorrow of the heart (Ps 13:2). Some cry all the time and others can't cry at all. We need a time of silent prayer in the presence of each other for these.

Thank You for listening and for loving us so much You will never leave us alone. We pray in the name of Jesus who bids us follow, and who still teaches us to pray together . . .

Comment: Next comes God's reassurance: God cares, listens, and loves. Nor does God ever leave us. This readies us to pray Jesus's prayer yet again: "Our Father, who art in heaven, hallowed be Thy name. Thy kingdom come, Thy will be done on earth as it is in heaven. Give us this day our daily bread. And forgive us our trespasses as we forgive those who trespass against us. And lead us—not into temptation, but deliver us from evil. For Thine is the kingdom, and the power, and the glory forever. Amen."

Transition to Prayer #4

Hi, my name is Steve Langhofer. I'm one of the pastors here at Resurrection. It is an amazing thing to realize how precious are these next moments of prayer to God. It is God's total delight to hear from us. Let's pray.

Comment: God is for us, not against us. God looks upon us as beloved daughters and sons. God cherishes our relationship more than anything. God wants our experience together in worship to be a time when we allow our tears to be wiped away, when we receive God's healing touch so that God's joy may be in us and so that our joy may be complete (John 15:11).

Pastoral and Lord's Prayers #4

O God of glory, Lord of love, You give us hope. You give us gladness and joy. You remove our sin and sadness. You drive out the darkness of our doubts. There is no one like You in Your greatness, Your strength, Your beauty. We bless Your name.

Comment: I begin by celebrating the attributes of God—glory, love, hope, gladness, joy. We find all these qualities in our Creator. I name God's nature: to reconcile, to bring light and life, to cast out fear, and to lift those who have been brought low. Only God can do this.

Thank You for Your presence with us and in us. Thank You for helping us not to be afraid when relationships are hard. For stopping us from

50

striking back when we are angry. For giving tolerance when we are with the intolerant. For showing us how to express appreciation even when we don't feel appreciated. Hear now our silent prayers of thanksgiving for all the ways You are present. (Pause.)

Comment: Gratitude rises in our hearts when in God's presence. We recall the ways God has helped us not to be afraid, not to feel threatened or become resentful, not to judge. Knowing we live in God's love frees us to love those who don't love back. And so, we say, "Thank You! Thank You for the abilities You give us."

Forgive us when we speak freely before we think, when we make racial comments that cause embarrassment and pain, or when we perpetuate hurtful stereotypes of those who believe differently. Forgive when we are unwilling to face our own prejudice. You have loved us beyond measure, O God, just the way we are. We know now it's our turn to love. Help us do a better job of it. Hear our silent prayers. (Pause.)

Comment: This week, a person of color shared how she felt hurt among friends who made insensitive racial remarks. They were unaware how their words led her to feel unsafe and disrespected. She actually withdrew for a time, wounded in spirit, uncertain how to help them understand her experience, questioning whether she would return.

We lift up those in need. For the victims of school shootings and their grieving families, for first responders, and for the shooters. For senior citizens who have been scammed out of their life savings. For those awaiting medical test results. For those who wrestle with addiction. For those searching for a reason to keep living. Hear our silent prayers. (Pause.)

Comment: There were so many people in need who I wanted to name. I face this every week. So, I selected a few whose need touched my heart most deeply, knowing that next week I can name the others. This particular week our nation once again experienced multiple school shootings. I made certain to include the shooters in the prayer. It has something to do with loving our enemies. A senior member of our congregation apologized for being unable to complete her financial pledge because she'd been scammed, and a young man who admitted himself to a detox unit and was deeply depressed had sent me a prayer request.

Hear our prayers, gracious God. Thank You for taking joy and delight in us every single day. Knowing this makes us strong. We pray in Jesus's name, the same Jesus who still teaches us to pray together . . .

Comment: I bring all the above back to God in preparation to pray Jesus's prayer. We stand before the One who says, "My grace is enough for you" (2 Cor 12:9). God's power is repeatedly made visible in our weakness. All creation groans to be set free from bondage (Rom 8:22). God believes in us enough, and through the Holy Spirit, God makes us strong enough to engage the struggle.

Transition to Prayer #5

Hi, my name is Steve Langhofer. I'm one of the pastors here at Resurrection. Whatever has been going on in your life this week, this is the time to bring it to God. The nice stuff and the not-so-nice stuff. Let's lift it to God.

Comment: "The nice stuff and the not-so-nice stuff": I like that phrase! Because Jesus came for those who need a physician (Matt 9:12). He came for the least, the last, and the lost (Matt 25:40). He embraced the pretty and the un-pretty. Amazing grace! Our people need that reminder regularly because just about everybody I know is more focused on their ugliness than on their beauty. Christ sees both and welcomes both (1 Sam 16:7).

Pastoral and Lord's Prayers #5

Because of Your love, O God, we lack nothing. You know what we need before we do, and You give it. Rest. Encouragement. Healing in our bodies. You stand with us in trouble. You hear us when we cry out. You forgive our wrongdoing. You bathe us with blessings. You keep us alive. Thank You, God. We praise You for Your love.

Comment: I was thinking about Psalm 139 when I wrote this first paragraph. God knows us inside and out, knows our actions, our thoughts, and our words. God envelops us with goodness; God is abounding in blessing and steadfast love. I love to start prayers this way.

O God of right relationships, direct us in paths of right living. O Master, let us walk with You, that Your goodness working in us may overcome evil. Help us understand ourselves that we may better understand each other. Plant Your stillness deep within, that when others are with us, they may grow calm. Help us rejoice gratefully with those who celebrate, sit patiently with those who grieve, listen carefully and learn from those who suffer. Forgive when we do not see the sacredness of strangers. Forgive when we draw unkind conclusions about people without even knowing them. Hear now our silent prayers. (Pause.)

Comment: The first two sentences were inspired by the hymn "O Master, Let Me Walk with Thee." The next sentence is a plea for self-understanding, which leads us to love our neighbor as we also strive to love ourselves. What a gift we will be, as we remain calm in a crisis with minimal anxiety. The next sentence is a paraphrasing of 1 Corinthians 12:26. I don't think there's anything wrong with borrowing great ideas from those who have prayed admirably before us. The sentence about strangers parallels Hebrews 13:1, and Jesus's reference to Himself as a stranger is in Matthew 25:36. We harbor way too much fear of strangers and do well to include them in every bidding prayer.

We pray for those who feel they've never been loved. For caregivers who are tired. For those who avoid sad friends because they don't know what to say. For those who feel they have failed someone dear. For those not taken seriously because they're either too young or too old or too different. For those who need a safe place to be themselves. Hear our silent prayers. (Pause.)

Comment: I'm repeating the theme of love throughout this prayer. Many might say they've never truly experienced love. So, I lift up caregivers who are trying to love, friends of grievers who don't know how to love, and those who believe they have failed at love. It is divine intervention that accepts us without condition (Rom 8:38-39).

O God, give us the same love—Your love—that was in Christ. The same mind. The same joy. The same Spirit. The same humility. The same servant's heart. The same readiness to empty ourselves that You may fill us. Unite us now in the same prayer that Jesus still gives us to pray together . . . .

Comment: Philippians 2 is triumphant in its portrait of Christ—his mind, his heart, his humility, his obedience. Through His Spirit He even helps us pray when we don't know how or think we've forgotten (Rom 8:26). "Our Father . . ."

Transition to Prayer #6

Hi, my name is Steve Langhofer. I'm one of the pastors here at Resurrection. Some weeks terrible things happen. Most weeks wonderful things happen. Whatever has happened to you this week, let's lift it together now in prayer.

Comment: God makes the sun shine on the evil and the good, and sends rain on the righteous and the unrighteous (Matt 5:45). I wrote this prayer the day after my niece was shot to death on a crowded downtown Kansas City street. I think I was still a bit numb. Everything seemed surreal. I was asked why I showed up for worship. I said there was no better place to be. And I thought everyone deserved to hear an honest prayer.

Pastoral and Lord's Prayers

O God, we are here to worship You. We worship You in good times, knowing nothing can separate us from Your love. Thank You for blessing us. Thank You for health, strength, wisdom, good humor, new beginnings, great sacrifices made for the benefit of others. For dear loved ones. For our country. For our church.

Comment: Even on this sad day, especially on this day, I needed to begin praying with praise for the true nature of God. Inseparable love. Blessing without ceasing. Full of glory, light and new life. Prodigal in justice. Good beyond our understanding. Beautiful. True. Joyous. Eternal. God's essential nature has not changed since yesterday.

We worship You in bad times knowing nothing can separate us from Your love. No matter how tragic, senseless, frightening, incomprehensible, heartbreaking, gut-wrenching, stupid, unspeakably maddening, wasteful, hurtful, unreal . . . we know in our hearts it cannot ultimately separate us from Your love. Thank You! Hear our silent prayers. (Pause.)

Comment: This was the hardest part of the prayer for me. Naming the evil without apology for sounding crude or irreverent. Drawing on the worst adjectives I could remember. But these are also true of God's nature: God is incarnational, agonizing, brokenhearted, suffering, crucified, descending into hell, resilient, redeeming, and inseparable from love. God's essential nature has not changed since yesterday.

We pray for the needs of others, and they are many. Help us show up exactly where You want us. Available. Open. Listening and looking. Teachable. Accountable. Compassionate to those in distress. Respectful of everyone. Seeking You in every encounter. Bearing witness to Your goodness. Pleasing You because we want to please You. Hear our silent prayers. (Pause.)

Comment: Then I knew it was time to draw attention away from ourselves. Lament is biblical, but we can stay there too long. We are not the only ones struggling. The sun shines and the rain falls on everyone, the good and the bad. But instead of generating a list of the needy, I thought it was important to focus on our relationship with God, and on God's need of us. It was important to be available and open, and to be listening and looking and teachable, so that we may grow wise. We must be accountable when we screw up without blaming someone else, and we must remain compassionate and respectful always. It is important to ask ourselves, "Where have I seen God today?"; we must find, and offer, hope.

Draw us close, O God. Draw all of us close, that where You are, we too may be. Feed us. Root us, ground us in You. Breathe Your breath upon us. Fill us fully, whether we ascend to heaven, or make our bed in the land of the dead or take the wings of the morning and settle at the farthest limits of the sea.

Comment: Here, I thought of scriptural images that help me, believing that they would help others. Such images included closeness to God and how Jesus promised this closeness in this life and in the next. Being nourished in Christ's Spirit and being rooted and grounded in His love were other images (Eph 3:16-17). I love how, on that first Easter morning, Jesus breathed on his disciples the breath of resurrected life (John 20:22). Breathe on me, O God! Help me inhale deeply of You lest I die (Ezek 37:4-5).

55

Receive our prayers today—You know what we mean; You know what we need; You know how we love You. And so, we worship You, in good times and in bad, in the name of Jesus, who still teaches us to pray together . . .

Comment: Here, I asked God to receive the offering of our prayers even as ancient priests did, standing before the altar and lifting the sacrifices of their people. Here, I was thinking about the Communion of Saints, those living and those dead, in whose presence we continue to worship and praise our God—no matter what.

Yes, I See What You Mean

I have shown you some of my own weekly worship prayers. I shared them, not to suggest that the way I write is best, but to clarify writing points with examples of integrating theology into pastoral work. I pray that you can, maybe, say, "Yes. I see what you mean!"

I hope this discipline helps you discover what works best for you. How has your belief system led you to pray? Sometimes figuring out what we don't believe is as crucial as knowing what we do believe. How do you assimilate your style of caring into leading others in prayer? Style is important. It makes us interesting. God help us if, when we pray, people start looking at their phones or doze off!

CHAPTER FIVE

Pastoral Prayers

In this section we offer prayers for you to use however you like. Adapt them or use them as they are for worship services. Read them devotionally. Study them as examples of what we've taught in this book.

You'll find prayers to use on important days of the Christian year: Advent, Christmas, Lent, Palm Sunday, Easter, Pentecost, World Communion Sunday, and All Saints Day.

Next, you'll find prayers for other special days: Mother's Day, Father's Day, Independence Day, Election Day, Veterans Day, Earth Day, Memorial Day, and New Year's Day or Eve.

Finally, you'll find prayers to use any day, any week of the year. Many of these are based on scripture passages, and we've included a handy index for those.

Many of these pastoral prayers lead into The Lord's Prayer. We use a capital "Y" as a reminder to ourselves that God is the being to whom we pray. God is the focus of these prayers, not us.

If you'd like to see more, we invite you to visit MinistryMatters.com.

Pastoral Prayers for the Church Year

Advent/Christmas

"Recognize Your Coming"

O God of divine illumination, we are Your grateful daughters and sons. God of ever-present Light, in You there is no darkness. We will praise You as long as we live, in every way we know how. We put our faith in You with child-like trust. Our hope in You rests secure.

O God who opens human hearts to receive You gladly, open ours. Remove our resistance. Enlighten our minds and brighten our eyes that we may recognize Your coming again in the Christ Child. For it is in Him that we find strength for our inner being. It is in Him that we are rooted and grounded in love. It is in Him that we are set free to accomplish abundantly far more for You than we ever could alone. It is because of Him that our hope overflows and we never lose heart.

We want to walk as children of Your light. We want to follow Jesus. Illumine us that we may teach Your truth. Comfort us that we may comfort those who mourn and encourage the poor in spirit. Shepherd us that we may shield the weak and bring back the lost. Forgive us that we may become forgivers. Humble us that we, like You, may humbly serve. Thank You, God, for Your grace. Forgive us for our lack of grace. Hear our silent prayers.

O God of the Advent promise, come. As in the past, and in the future, be with us now. We, Your grateful daughters and sons, are so happy to call You our God. Receive the prayers of our hearts and bless them, even as we bless You in every way we know how. We offer them in the name of Jesus as we again pray His prayer: "Our Father who art in heaven, hallowed be thy name. Thy kingdom come, thy will be done on earth as it is in heaven. Give us this day our daily bread. And forgive us our trespasses as we forgive those who trespass against us. And lead us—not into temptation, but deliver us from evil. For thine is the kingdom, and the power, and the glory forever. Amen."

"Coming to Us Once More"

Eternal God who was, and is, and ever shall be, we praise You in this Advent season for coming to us once more. We praise You for being our God and claiming us as Your people. We praise You for Your living Word revealed in scripture, promised through prophecy, celebrated in song, made flesh in Jesus Christ.

Thank You for our friends and family, for our health and our homes. Thank You for our country, in which we live free from fear, free from want, free from oppression. Thank You for Your saving grace when we wander in darkness and doubt, and for confidence in faith where we cannot see. Thank You for believing in us when we find it hard to believe in ourselves. Hear our silent prayers of praise and thanksgiving. (Pause.)

We pray for the homeless and hungry. We pray for those who are angry and finding it hard to forgive. We pray for those who have lost their dreams and are hungry for hope. O come, O come, Emmanuel, God be with us yet again. Ransom us from our captivity to false beliefs and un-healthy behaviors. Create in us new hearts and renewed commitments. Restore us with Your Holy Spirit in the name and power of Jesus, the same Jesus who still teaches us to pray together . . .

"Making Yourself Known"

O God, who makes Yourself known to us in Jesus, who is our Light and in whom there is no darkness at all, we praise You! O Creator of the ends of the earth, the stars, planets, and heavens above, we worship You!

Thank You for the way You bless us. Thank You for celebrating our glad-ness and consoling us in our sadness. Thank You for setting us free from anxiety and fear. Thank You for protecting us, for hemming us in, be-hind and before, so we don't unravel. When we are bruised, You soothe us. When we despair, You give us hope. When we are restless, You help us find our rest in You.

We confess *that* in us, which separates us from You—our thoughts, our actions, our lack of action. Our resistance to the changes You ask us to make. Our doubting You. Our distressing You. Please, forgive us.

Forgive us. Thank You for continuing to affirm the best in us, in Your mercy and grace, without shaming the worst in us. Hear now our silent prayers. (Silence.)

We pray for the poor and homeless, and for those who are barely making it financially. For those who are sick, or hospitalized, or in rehab. We pray for those who have died, or who grieve, and for all of those in need of Your healing touch. For those who have been harmed and those who harmed them. For appropriate ways to express our anger. Hear now our silent prayers. (Silence.)

We pray in this season of Advent, as we prepare for Your coming, for a season of expectation and promise. We pray in the name of Jesus, who shines in our hearts and minds, who shepherds our souls, and who still teaches us to pray together . . .

"No Darkness—At All"

O come, o come, Lord Jesus. Make Your advent here. We love You. We worship You. We want to follow You. We want to live in Your light, for in You there is NO darkness at all.

O Jesus, who had compassion for crowds in the desert, we, too, come to You hungry. Hungry for Your healing, Your nourishment, Your encouragement, Your attention. Feed us with the living bread of Your presence that we may be filled. And with the leftovers, use us to feed others.

We pray for our leaders in Washington, and here at home. We remember the poor and homeless, those at war, and those without a country. We remember the sick, and those who grieve. Those who battle depression and addiction. Those who find it hard to believe in anything, or anyone.

We confess that we want to fix things that cannot be fixed. We lose control, and it frightens us. So, we strike out. We do things we don't mean to and say things we cannot take back. We make mistakes. We forget our manners. We are sorry. Please forgive us. Hear now our silent prayers. (Silence.)

Fill us with hope. Let Your joy be our strength. When we are down, give us a fighting spirit to get back up. Grant us faith that we may endure, and endure so that we may lack in nothing.

O come, o come, Lord Jesus. Make Your advent here. Let us live in Your light, for in You there is NO darkness at all. We give You our prayers, remembering how even You underwent great suffering and rejection, and were killed. But after three days You rose again, triumphant, and still to this day, you teach us to pray together . . .

"Deliver Us"

Mighty God, everlasting Father, Wonderful Counselor, we need You. We need You to set us free from all that frightens us. Free us from anything harmful, from that which makes for restlessness and trouble. Release us from bondage. Repair our damage. Restore our well-being. Refresh our spirits.

Deliver us, through the power of Your Holy Spirit, from all that robs us of joy. Protect us. Lead us. Raise us on wings like eagles that we may soar high and far.

Save us from darkness that we may walk as children in Your light. Make us glad to trust Your good intentions, remembering that if You are for us, no one can successfully be against us—save us from our doubts. Hear our silent prayers. (Silence.)

We pray for *others* who need You: the sick, those in prison, strangers among us who need a friend, those with broken hearts who need Your touch, and those without power who suffer violence and oppression. Set them free. Deliver them. Help them know You are their Advocate, too, and save them from their doubts.

We all need You, gracious God, You who abolish death and bring forth life. We praise and honor You this day through Jesus Christ, the risen One, who still teaches us to pray together . . .

61

"Bring Us Home"

O glorious God of peace, You are greatly to be praised! You are gracious and merciful, slow to anger, abounding in steadfast love. When we stumble into dark places we never intended, we know we can always come home. You are our patient, persistent, prodigal Father who sees us stumbling in the distance, then runs to embrace, kiss, and celebrate us—even in our unworthiness. We admire Your grace-filled spirit, O God, and are humbled by it. We praise You for the way You make peace.

Teach us, if You would, how to live peaceably with ourselves and each other. If someone is angry, help us not respond defensively, but to listen and seek understanding. If someone is hurting, remind us how You have consoled us in our affliction, that we might offer consolation to them. If someone is oppressed and needs an advocate, grant us courage to stand with them, being strong, clear, and unafraid. Make us instruments of Your holy peace. Hear our silent prayers, now, for all who need to hear good news, to be healed, to be set free. (Silence.)

O come, O come, Emmanuel; God be with us again. Like a fragrant rose, tender and sweet, ever blooming in a dry and weary land, bloom brightly in our midst that there may be joy and singing. Dispel our darkness; deliver us from sin and death; save us now. Fix our eyes upon Jesus, who comes to love, serve, and to proclaim Your favor; our Wonderful Counselor, our Mighty God, who still teaches us to pray together . . .

"Persistent Presence"

Emmanuel, God with us, we come to worship You! We rejoice because of the great things You have done! We praise You for cheering our spirits, for dispersing the gloomy clouds of our nights! You bring us light and life. No one is like You!

Thank You for all You give us that is good, and right, and true. We're so glad You have come and have promised never to leave. Thank You for making Yourself known in the Christ Child, the Prince of Peace, and for bringing us into Your Presence. Though we fall short of Your dreams,

You think well of us, and You know us better than anyone. So, we trust You, we feel safe in You.

Forgive us when we cause others to feel unsafe, for when we create mistrust. Forgive for insisting on our own way, for cheating by not telling the whole truth. Forgive us when we discount the legitimate needs of others. Remind us that we're all pretty much the same inside. Hear now our silent prayers. (Silence.)

We pray that we may be advocates of justice for those oppressed. Make us good stewards of the earth, of water and air. May we be humble, yet earnest, evangelists to those who do not know You. We pray for the poor and for those without work. For the sick and those in need of healing. For those who are sad over being separated from loved ones through death, or divorce, or family disagreements. We remember Your promise to comfort those who mourn. Hear now our silent prayers. (Silence.)

Make us strong in You, that we may serve You with enthusiasm and in singleness of heart. Reinforce our undying love for You in Christ Jesus, born of Mary, the One who still teaches us to pray together . . .

"We Trust You"

Loving God, thank You for being who You are. We lift up our eyes to You, the one from whom our help comes. We lift up our eyes to You, who made heaven and earth. You keep us from all evil. You watch over our going out and our coming in. We have our grounding in You. We live in Your shelter. We abide in Your shadow. Thank You for the good things You do for us. Thank You for loving us no matter what. Thank You for helping us trust You.

We believe. Please forgive our unbelief. Forgive us when we take Your generous gift of faith and turn it into little faith. Forgive us when we doubt You and, instead, focus on the darkness. Hear now our silent confessions. (Silence.) Prepare us in this Advent season to receive the gift of Your Christ Child, that His hope and His peace may live in our hearts.

Hear our prayers for those who are ill, for those who grieve, for those who don't know how they're going to pay their bills, for the lonely and the alienated, and those trying to forgive. We hold up to You, silently now, those in need. (Silence.)

We trust You, God, with the most private apsects of our lives. We place in Your hands those most dear because we know they are safe and we know that You are always working for good. Hear our prayers, in the name of Jesus Christ, the One who still teaches us to pray together . . .

"Cheer Our Spirits"

Emmanuel, God with us, we come to worship You! We rejoice because of the great things You have done! We praise You for cheering our spirits, for dispersing the gloomy clouds of our nights! You bring us light and life. No one is like You!

Thank You for all You give us that is good and right and true. We're so glad You have come and promise never to leave. Thank You for making Yourself known in the Christ Child, the Prince of Peace, and bringing us into Your Presence. Though we fall short of Your dreams, You think well of us, and You know us better than anyone. So, we trust You, we feel safe in You.

Forgive us when we cause others to feel unsafe, for when we create mistrust. Forgive for insisting on our own way, for cheating by not telling the whole truth. Forgive when we discount the legitimate needs of others. Remind us that we're all pretty much the same inside. Hear now our silent prayers. (Silence.)

We pray that we may be advocates of justice for those oppressed. Make us good stewards of the earth, of water and air. May we be humble, yet earnest, evangelists to those who do not know You. We pray for the poor and for those without work. For the sick and those in need of healing. For those who are sad over being separated from loved ones through death, or divorce, or family disagreements. We remember Your promise to comfort those who mourn. Hear now our silent prayers. (Silence.)

Make us strong in You that we may serve You with enthusiasm, in singleness of heart. Reinforce our undying love for You in Christ Jesus, born of Mary, the One who still teaches us to pray together . . .

"Stronger Than We Know"

O glorious and blessed God, maker of heaven and earth and sea and sky and all that is in them, we come into Your presence with thanksgiving and praise. We worship You with gladness. Thank You for the good news of great joy in the Christ Child of Bethlehem. Because He is with us, we are not afraid!

Thank You for the gift of Your grace in this season and all year long. Thank you for daily health and security. For friends and loved ones. For newborn babies and the laughter of children at play. For the companionship of our pets. Thank You for watching over our sleep and our dreams, always guarding our minds and hearts. Thank You for making us strong in ways we did not know we could be strong, and for helping us endure with patience that which must be endured.

Thank You for Your forgiveness when we make poor decisions, when we accuse someone falsely, or when we thoughtlessly criticize those whom we do not understand. Forgive when we forget the poor, those who are sick or in prison or oppressed, those whose hearts are broken. Please understand when our disappointment in You causes us to lose hope. Hear now our silent prayers of confession. (Silence.)

Thank You for Your steadfast love, and for Your advent among us once more. We worship You. In Your presence, Emmanuel, we find fullness of joy and, because You are with us, we are not afraid! We offer these prayers in the name of Jesus, in whom we find our true rest, and the one who still teaches us to pray together . . .

"Make Smooth Our Rough Places"

O great God of promise, You have come to us in Christ whose birth the angels sing! Your glory has appeared, and we have seen it together! You have anointed us with Your Holy Spirit, and we are filled with joy!

We confess we need help changing our hearts and lives. We criticize others too much. We envy others too much. We hold onto resentment too much. Straighten out our crookedness and make smooth our rough places. Hear now our silent prayers. (Silence.)

We pray for the earth and its well-being. For leaders who need guidance. For all who need work. For those who don't have a home. For those who suffer and those who grieve. For those whose souls are troubled. For those who need to forgive. For those who have done evil, and we ask that You convict their hearts to repentance, as we recognize that the capacity for sin that we see in others also resides in us. Hear now our silent prayers. (Silence.)

O God of mercy and grace, help us practice self-control and make us kind. Give us patience that we may persevere. May we be generous and rich in faith. May we be people who take delight in each other, even as You take delight in us. We pray in the name of Jesus, who was born in Bethlehem and grew strong in wisdom, humility, and obedience, who was crucified, but whom You raised from the dead, the same Jesus, the same Jesus who still teaches us to pray together . . .

"Where Else to Turn"

We come to worship You, Jesus. The angels sang at Your birth. We join them, and the shepherds, too. We join the sheep, cattle, and the donkey—all making their animal sounds. We like to think that they were all pleased to be in Your presence. We are! We come to worship You, Jesus, because You come to us.

Thank You for the faith You give, for teaching us to trust. We really want to believe in You. Help our unbelief. Please understand when we resist. Is it our arrogance that gets in the way; we think we're too smart to need You. Or perhaps it is our low self-esteem, that we don't feel worthy? Thank You for faithfully guiding us in Your direction when we don't know where else to turn.

We pray for those who suffer, those who are sad or afraid, those who feel they have lost themselves. We don't always know how to help each other, so encourage us when we try but fail. Forgive us if we've done anything this week that has gotten in Your way. Hear now our silent prayers. (Silence.) We know that when we are at our weakest, then You are at Your strongest. And so, we have hope. Let Your all-sufficient grace dwell in us. Fill our mouths with laughter, our lips with shouts of joy.

We worship You, Jesus. We lift our voices with the angels because You come to us. We are pleased to be in Your presence. At Your birth, You were wrapped in bands of cloth and laid in a manger. And at Your death, You were wrapped in a purple cloak, a crown of thorns, and laid in a tomb. Yet even this could not stop You. You defeated sin, and darkness, and death so that nothing could ever separate us from Your love. And still to this day You teach us to pray together . . .

"Making Noble Efforts"

All glory be to You, O God, as You come to us in the Christ Child, the babe, the son of Mary. At his birth You proved that Your steadfast love and mercy would never end, but would be renewed every morning and every night. At his birth, You shone light into our darkness, and promised compassion over all You had made. At his birth You became flesh, living among us, bringing glimpses of Your glory and glad tidings of Your grace.

Forgive us, Lord Jesus, when we do not recognize or receive You in the babies and noisy children around us. Forgive us when we see people hungry and thirsty and fail to feed them or give them drink. Or when we decline to reach out to those who are sick or in prison, or those who simply need someone to listen to them. Forgive us when we shun the stranger or judge the refugee and do not see them as members of Your family, for whom You came at Christmas. Hear now our silent prayers.

O God, in Your mercy, grant us grace. We pray for our loved ones, that they may be healthy, happy, and whole. We pray for the ill, the grieving, the lonely. We pray for those making noble efforts to stay sober. We pray for those refusing to speak to each other. We pray for those desperate for a good night's sleep. We pray for those enduring the holidays, and those who need assurance that second chances in life are real.

O God, in Your mercy, grant us grace. Receive our prayers and our praise as we come before You on bended knees. All glory, all honor be to You, whose steadfast love and mercy never end but are renewed every morning and every night. We lift all this to You in the name of the

Bethlehem babe, the son of Mary, Jesus our Christ, who still teaches us to pray together . . .

"Joyful and Triumphant?"

Almighty God, creator of heaven and earth, we come before You humble and transparent. "O Come all ye faithful, joyful and triumphant?" Well . . . we come *trying* to be faithful, wishing we were more joyful, knowing very little about how to live triumphant. We come singing, perhaps not always so sweetly, but offering You glory in the highest as best we know how, imagining angels in heaven eagerly singing with us.

We bow on bended knee alongside adoring shepherds who embraced Your arrival as a babe, innocent and vulnerable. We love You, God, for the way You love us. We trust that You intend nothing but good, steadfastly so. We are learning You do some of Your best work when we stumble and lose our way.

Save us, God. Shine Your light into our darkness, that we may not be overcome. Make Your love complete in us that we may give it away to those who have not known love, and some days that's not easy to do. Help us. Hear our silent prayers now as we open our hearts confidently before You. (Silence.)

O God, come and be with us. Forgive, restore, draw us to Yourself. Prepare us once more for the glad celebration of Your birth. Keep us ever sensitive and available to those who are ill, to the poor, the oppressed, those addicted and those desperate for justice and peace. Raise them up, and us, with all Your people that we may wait with expectant hope for Your return through Jesus Christ, the same Jesus, risen from the dead, who still teaches us to pray together . . .

"For Whom This Time Is Difficult"

O glorious and blessed God, we give You thanks, and praise Your name. We declare Your steadfast love in the morning, and Your faithfulness by night. You make us glad for Your reconciling work among us, and we sing for joy! From everlasting to everlasting, You are God, our Refuge and Rock!

Help us be still in Your presence and grow strong, depending on Your strength and not our own. Cast out our sin, enter in and be born in us this day.

We confess we are scared far too much of the time. Free us from fear and worry. You've known us since before we were born, and you love us exactly as You've made us. You know us inside out. We belong to You. We are secure in You. You are in charge. Help us remember. Keep us close. Help us not miss out on Your grace. Save us from disbelief. Hear now our silent prayers as we open our hearts to You. (Silence.)

Thank You for the blessings of this Christmas season. Thank You for health and home, for parents, for children, for sisters and brothers and good friends. Thank You for our baptism and place in Your Church. We pray for those who are sad and for whom this time is difficult. We pray for the sick, the poor, those in prison, those at war.

Pour out Your grace upon all Your creation, O God of glory, O Prince of Peace. We ask this in the name of Jesus Christ, our Emmanuel, Son of Righteousness, Light and Life to us all, and who still teaches us to pray together . . .

"Beacons of Justice"

Eternal God, from whom we come, in whom we live and move and have our being, to whom we return, You bring us such good news at Christmas! Your gifts are many and full of wonder: glory, peace, mercy, reconciliation from sin, light and life, healing.

You are so pleased with us as daughters and sons that You come to us in a manger in the little town of Bethlehem, and shine in our dark streets with everlasting light. You have taken flesh upon Yourself, become one with us, one of us, that we may be one with You. Surprising and gracious God, we are pleased to dwell with You, too. Thank You for being our God, and for choosing us as Your people.

69

Thank You for casting out our sin and entering in. Do make us beacons of Your justice and defenders of those for whom there is no room—the homeless and hungry, the unemployed and uninsured, the imprisoned, and the victims of prejudice and persecution. We pray for all in need— the sick, the dying, those grieving, and those working hard to overcome addictions. We lift them to You, silently. (Silence.)

Let there be joy in our world today . . . joy that You have come to us again . . . joy that all nations may rise and join the triumph of the skies . . . joy that You enter in still where meek souls receive You . . . joy that You are here, that You are as near as our breathing . . . joy that we know You and are found in You through Jesus, our Emmanuel, to whom be glory and honor and praise forever and ever . . . joy that each day You open our eyes to His presence, and prayerfully intercede in and through and for us, teaching us even now to pray together . . .

"Not Everyone Sings"

O God our Creator, Redeemer, and Sustainer, thank You for Your good gift of life. Thank You for loving us with persistent resolve. Thank You for strength and courage sufficient for today's brightness and the shadows of tonight. Thank You for knowing us by name and claiming us as Your own.

When we go through difficult times You are with us, so we are not overcome. Though wounded and scarred, You heal and make us whole. The rivers do not overwhelm; the fires cannot consume, for You are God, the Holy One, our Savior. There is pure joy in this world because of Your coming at Christmas—all heaven and nature sing Your praise, and so do we!

But not everyone is singing. Many are hurting, discouraged, and trying desperately to push back darkness, but are unable to do so alone. Help them, Lord. Help us help them. Give them hope, peace, joy: May the whole world see Your long-awaited light. We now lift to You silently all who are in need. (Silence.)

Forgive us, God, when we fail to appreciate the struggles of others and are too quick to judge. Grant us understanding hearts and generous

70

spirits. Make us willing to do the things that make for peace. This we ask in Jesus's name, the same Jesus who taught then and teaches us to pray together . . .

"Joy to Our World"

O God, who brings joy to our world, who makes Yourself known to us in Jesus who is our Light and in whom there is no darkness at all, we praise You! O Creator of the ends of the earth, the stars and planets and heavens above, we worship You!

Thank You for the way You bless us. Thank You for celebrating our gladness and consoling us in our sadness. Thank You for setting us free from anxiety and fear. Thank You for protecting us, for hemming us in, behind and before, so we don't unravel. When we are bruised, You soothe us. When we despair, You give us hope. When we are restless, You help us find our rest in You.

We confess *that* in us, which separates us from You: our thoughts, our actions, our inaction. Our resistance to the changes You ask us to make. Our doubting You. Our distressing You. Please, forgive us. Forgive us. Thank You for continuing to affirm the best in us, in Your mercy and grace, without shaming the worst in us. Hear now our silent prayers. (Silence.)

We pray for the poor and homeless, and for those barely making it financially. For those who are sick, or hospitalized, or in rehab, or who have died, or who grieve, and for all in need of Your healing touch. For those who have been harmed and those who harmed them, and for appropriate ways to express our anger. Hear now our silent prayers. (Silence.)

We pray in this season of Christmas as we celebrate Your coming, a season of expectation and promise. We pray in the name of Jesus who shines in our hearts and minds, who shepherds our souls, and who still teaches us to pray together . . .

"Making Home Here"

O Jesus at Christmas, we come to worship You. We come to praise You. We come to adore You on bended knee. We honor You. We declare Your glory. We bless Your name. O Jesus at Christmas, let heaven and nature sing!

Thank You for making Your home here. Thank You for helping us recognize and receive You. Thank You for enabling us to believe, that we may become one with You.

Forgive us when we do not perceive Your presence, when we fail to acknowledge and honor Your Holy Spirit in each other. Forgive us when we underestimate our importance to You. Impress upon us Your love, and forgive us when we doubt the reason You came to be with us. Hear now our silent prayers. (Silence.)

We pray for those who suffer pain. For those whose minds and hearts are troubled. For those who wish to die. For the poor. For those in prison. For those who do not yet know You, but who need You.

As we prepare for 2022, we ask that You grow us closer to You than we've ever been. Rest Your hand upon us. Make us strong with Your strength, wise in Your ways, patient with each other and with ourselves. Keep us humble. Keep us in good humor. Let Your peace and Your joy surprise us.

O Jesus at Christmas, we worship You, we adore You on bended knees, let heaven and nature sing! O child born at Christmas, O Savior raised at Easter, we pray to You, who still teaches us to pray together . . .

Lent

"Humility in Jesus"

Eternal God—the One from whom we come, in whom we live, and to whom we will return—love divine, joy of heaven, we bless You this day.

We praise You for Your greatness and glory, Your wonder and wisdom, Your exceeding excellence, Your purity and perfection.

We praise You for the humble way You came to us in Jesus Christ, who emptied Himself, being born in human form, becoming our servant, remaining obedient unto death on a cross, that we might look upon Him and see You.

Thank You that our sin and brokenness are met with His mercy and grace. Thank You for touching us through Him when we need healing and strength. Thank You for His words of acceptance and inclusion when we feel like outsiders. Thank You for His Spirit of joy and delight in the presence of new life and renewed hope. Thank You for our ability to trust in His transforming power even as we suffer and confront mystery. Thank You for His invitation to pray for loved ones and friends, for strangers and enemies. Hear now our silent prayers. (Silence.)

O love divine, all loves excelling, receive our prayers. Receive our love, and our blessing, and our praise. Breathe Your Spirit into our hearts once more. Fill us with Your peace and patience, Your kindness and generosity. Anoint us as Your ambassadors of reconciliation. Remind us again that we belong to Jesus Christ. Keep us close to Him always. Guard and guide us by His Spirit, even now as we pray again as Jesus still teaches us . . .

"When We Disappoint Ourselves"

O God our Creator who has given us life, thank You for our hearts that beat and our lungs that breathe. Thank You for pouring Yourself into us that we might know You. Thank You for Your Spirit, and Your strength. Thank You for each other. Thank You for Your love that helps us bear, and believe and hope and endure all things.

Forgive us when we disappoint You, when we disappoint ourselves. Forgive us when we are secretly content that someone else has to struggle, or when we see an opponent suffer and we take delight. Soften our hearts. Enlarge our capacity to care deeply when anyone is in pain, or hungry, or afraid. Hear our silent prayers. (Silence.)

73

Restore to us right relationships. Rekindle within us Your gift of compassion. Teach us again to rejoice when anyone is honored, to be glad at someone else's good fortune, that there may be no dissension among us. Make us one with each other in Christ Jesus.

Bring us once more to the foot of His cross. Help us humbly bow. Drive out any darkness within and draw us into His peace. Lift our eyes to meet His. Open our hearts and hands to receive His mercy, His unlimited grace, that by His wounds we may be healed.

Hear our prayers, O God. We lift them to You in Jesus's name as we join in the prayer, which he still teaches us to pray . . .

"Claimed, Embraced and Kissed"

O God, in Your steadfast, amazing love You search us, and know us. You are acquainted with all our ways, and You love us still! You blot out our transgressions. You wash us from sin. You create in us clean hearts. You put new and right spirits within. We worship You, we sing to You, we praise You.

You proudly keep claiming us as daughters and sons. You embrace us with a holy kiss. You rebuild our confidence. You help us live worthy lives pleasing in Your sight. You teach us endurance, so we don't quit when it's best that we persevere. You keep our sense of humor fresh. You take away our fear. You help us cry when our hearts break. You hold us close in our sorrow at night. You give us joy in the morning. We worship You; we sing to You; we praise You.

You elect us for ministry and inspire us to serve. You give us hearts big with compassion for those overlooked or forgotten or oppressed, and a readiness to act. You give us wisdom to sort out what's important and what's not. You remind us that knowing we belong to You, whether we live or whether we die, everything else falls into place. Hear, O Lord, our silent prayers of confession and thanksgiving. (Silence.)

We worship You; we sing to You; we praise You. O God who makes light shine out of darkness, who in all things works for good, who promises to draw us to Yourself in the cross of Jesus Christ, graciously receive the prayers of our hearts this day. Make us one with our risen Lord who still teaches us to pray together . . .

"Steadfast, Loyal, Endless"

O great and faithful God, thank You for Your dependability, Your steadfastness, Your loyalty, Your reliability, Your truthfulness and trustworthiness, Your fidelity, Your unchanging love. Thank You for Your understanding, Your patience, Your forgiveness, Your endless grace. We worship You. We praise You. We love You.

We confess to You, O God. We are quick to make judgment. We are short with our tolerance. We have broken promises. We exclude those You include. We run out of grace. We want too much to be the center of attention. Forgive us. Hear now our silent prayers. (Silence.)

We pray for people who die in air crashes, and for their loved ones who grieve. Comfort them. We pray for our sisters and brothers who are wounded and murdered while worshipping and for those who execute that violence. We pray for the sick, for those struggling to resist temptation, for family members who don't speak to one another, for our leaders in Washington and in our denomination. Hear our silent prayers for those in need. (Silence.)

We surrender our lives to You. Take over. Take control. Shepherd us. Lead us. Teach us. Hold and mold us. Shape us according to Your will. Give us each the fruits of Your Spirit, for the good of all: wisdom, knowledge, faith, gifts of healing, serving, encouraging, teaching, leading, witnessing. Each of us is different, yet together we are made into one body in You. We pray this in the name of Jesus, the Crucified One, who lives in us and who shows us how to live, and who still teaches us to pray together . . .

"O Jesus, Hover over Us"

O Jesus, who was before all things, whose name is above all things, and in whom all things hold together, we praise You. You triumphed over the grave. You died that we might live. Thank You.

Thank You for our loved ones. Bless and keep them safe. Thank You for daily health, and for signs of new life in nature, in little children, and in our grateful hearts. Thank You for the intimacy of Your presence and the quiet sighs of Your Spirit.

We confess that we work hard but often with little sense of accomplishment. We talk with each other but often don't really connect. We engage in activities that leave us feeling empty inside. We worry about our aging bodies. We're more afraid than we want to admit. And sometimes when we pray about these things, we wonder whether they matter to You. Hear now our silent prayers. (Silence.)

We pray for the poor and oppressed. We pray for those who are ill and those who sorrow. We pray for our country that our political divisiveness may be minimized. We pray for our elected leaders that they may govern with integrity and care. We pray for courageous students who march in the streets that violence may end and that their classrooms may become safe again. Hear now our silent prayers. (Silence.)

O Jesus who is one with the Father and the Holy Spirit, hover over us. Fill us with Yourself. Make us eager to tell others how You make all things new. And teach us once more how You would have us pray together . . .

"When Days and Nights Are Hard"

We praise You, God Almighty, author of creation, Lord of sea and sky. You make the stars at night. You make the darkness bright. You are our health and salvation. You bear us on eagles' wings. You enfold us in Your care. You sustain us with goodness and truth.

Thank You for being who You are, and for doing what You do. Some days wear us to a frazzle, but You revive our strength. Some nights go on endlessly, but You give us enough rest for tomorrow. Some hours are so lonely, but You never withdraw. Some tasks seem overwhelming, but You say to us, "Fear not! Take my hand!"

Thank You for Your church and the home You give. Thank You for ministry, Your calling us to share in it, and for Your Spirit, who equips and sends us to serve. Thank You for our baptism and Holy Communion through which You give us identity and feed us on the journey.

We confess our slowness to trust You. We forget Your abiding presence. We dwell too much on our inadequacies and compare ourselves too often to others. We neglect the poor, the sick, those in prison, and the oppressed. We have not done a good job of holding Your people in our hearts. Hear now our silent confessions. (Silence.)

We are no longer our own, O Lord, but Yours. Make us truly repentant. Give us hearts for love alone and let nothing in all of creation come between us. Let joy and gladness be found in us, and the voice of song. We ask this in the name of Jesus, who has risen triumphantly from the dead, and who still teaches us to pray together . . .

"All Creatures Lift Your Voices"

We praise You, Creator God, for You have made us and we are Yours. We praise You with brother sun and sister moon. We praise You with the wind and air, and clouds and rain. We praise You in the morning and the evening and midday, too. We worship and honor You. We glorify and bless You.

Thank You, God, for caring about the poor, the sick, those in prison, and those heartbroken with grief. Reassure us that You Yourself agonize when nations and countries are torn apart by war, and that You hurt, too, when people are exploited and abused. Give us hearts that care like You care.

Give us permission to argue with You about injustice when we see it. Help us not put distance between us when we're mad at You. Receive our complaints—whether about a child's death, a plane crash, a cancer diagnosis, a crime somebody got away with—receive our complaints, and after we've gotten it out of our system, redirect us in more useful ways. Hear, now, our laments and confessions. Please understand us and forgive us, as we pray silently. (Silence.)

Thank You for Your sustaining grace, and for pouring Yourself into our lives through Your Spirit in Christ Jesus. Sometimes we don't feel like we know very much. But we know You love us, and that's enough. You have made us, and we are Yours. Knowing that You are with us no matter what is enough to keep us encouraged. Do use us to encourage others. All this we pray in Jesus's name, our risen Savior, who still teaches us to pray together . . .

"When Relationships Fail"

O God of goodness, O Jesus of all compassion, O Holy Spirit of grace, we worship You. Your all-excelling love knows no bounds. We praise You, we honor You. Thank You for Your blessings in good times and bad, and for being who You are.

Have mercy upon us. We have strayed from Your way. We have hurt others when it was unnecessary. We have neglected to do what would make it easier for someone else. We have thought too highly of ourselves. We have also thought too poorly of ourselves. Forgive us and cleanse us from our sin, as we lift our confession to You in silence. (Silence.)

Deliver us from our fears. Save us from shame. Change our hearts. Make us more like You. Plant new and steadfast spirits within. Satisfy us with living water. Feed us with the bread of Your presence. Strengthen us in our inner being with power through Your Spirit. Root us, ground us, and dwell in our hearts through faith. Breathe upon us Your breath once more, that we may know Your peace.

O Lord, let us walk with You. Let us be of service to You, encourage somebody for You, give somebody hope because of You. We pray for the sick and those who grieve. We pray for the poor, those in prison, those at war, and for those who have no country to call home. We pray for the earth, the air, the wheat fields and the forests. We pray for happy relationships, and for those who divorce. Bless and keep all Your creation,

O God of second chances. We ask this in the name of Jesus, who still teaches us to pray together . . .

Palm Sunday

"Palm Branches and Passion"

Holy God, eternal and loving God, You are worthy of all glory, honor, and praise. We bless You; we celebrate You. We exalt and hallow Your name. We respect You, for You are full of wonder. We sing of Your graciousness because You have reconciled the world to Yourself. "Hosanna in the highest heaven!" You have taken our pain, our brokenness and sorrow upon Yourself in Jesus Christ and saved us, making us one with You. Nothing can ever again separate us.

Thank You, God, for Your faithfulness to all creation. Thank You for executing justice for the oppressed, for feeding the hungry, for setting prisoners free, for opening the eyes of the blind, and for lifting up those who are bowed down. Thank You for gathering the outcasts to Yourself, for healing the brokenhearted and binding up their wounds. Thank You for giving the world hope, thank You for giving *us* hope, for all the ways You touch and make us whole. Hear now our silent prayers of praise and thanksgiving. (Silence.)

Forgive us for taking Your love that we know in Jesus for granted. Draw us close to the footsteps of Jesus this holy week. Let us not only wave palm branches in His honor but also join His inner circle at supper on the night of His betrayal. May we kneel in the garden with Him, sharing His obedience to Your will. Make us able to stand trembling before His cross as He empties Himself in voluntary suffering. Help us to weep as He is carried to His grave. Draw us to Jesus this holy week, O God, the same Jesus who still teaches us to pray together . . .

"All Glory and Honor"

Hosanna in the highest to You, eternal God! Glory and honor forever be Yours! O may we ever praise You with heart and life and voice, and in Your blessed presence eternally rejoice! For health and strength, we thank You. For sustaining us day and night, we praise You. For being ever available, for being our perpetual encourager, the One who ceaselessly ensures that we have everything we need. We worship and adore You.

You comfort us in our losses and protect us in danger. You help us trust You when we are afraid. You let nothing come between us and Your love. Because of the suffering, death, and triumphant resurrection of Jesus, all that goes wrong, all our sin and brokenness, all our worries and confusion are overcome by Your great power. You are gracious, steadfast, patient. You understand and forgive. You never abandon, quit, or give up on us. Glory be to You, O God! Hosanna in the highest!

Forgive us when we do not love You with all our hearts. Forgive us when we don't do Your will or keep Your law, or when we don't love our neighbors and make their needs a higher priority. Forgive us for not taking better care of ourselves. Hear our confessions in silence. (Silence.)

Hear our prayers for the poor, the unemployed, the powerless, those dying and those grieving, those sick or hospitalized or homebound, those living with pain, and for those at war and returning from war. We lift up silently all who are in need. (Silence.)

May we ever praise You, glorious God, with heart and life and voice, and in Your blessed presence eternally rejoice! We pray in the name and Spirit of Jesus, who taught us then and who teaches us now to pray together . . .

"Hosanna! Save Us"

O God our Maker, Creator of the universe, who sets the sun and moon and stars in their place, we worship You. God of majesty and mercy, we glorify Your holy name! Teach us to delight in You. Make us happy to be like trees planted by streams of water yielding fruit for You, like palm trees waving our branches in praise to You: Hosanna! Blessings in the highest heaven!

Help us trust You. Let the light of Your face shine on us. Put gladness in our hearts, that when we lie down at night we sleep in peace and rise refreshed eager to serve You once more. Thank You for daily health. Thank You for loved ones—keep them safe; bless them. Thank You for the earth, its beauty, its bounty, its resilience—heal it where it has suffered harm.

Forgive us when we do not do Your will or keep Your law. Forgive us when we do not love You with all our hearts, or fail to love our neighbor or ourselves. Forgive us when we fail to be a community of grace. Hear now our silent confessions. (Silence.)

We pray for the poor, the unemployed, those dying and grieving; for those hospitalized or homebound; those at war and those who are its victims. We pray for relationships damaged beyond repair; for those convinced they are unworthy of love; for those who have been lied to so many times they find it impossible to trust; for those who haven't experienced joy for so long that they have forgotten what it is.

Pour out Your joy upon us all. Set us free from fear. Shine light into our darkness. Give us eyes to recognize You, hearts to receive You, and voices to speak hope to those who do not yet know You. Hosanna! Save us, Lord! We humbly ask this in the name of Jesus, who still teaches us to pray together . . .

Easter

"Let Praises Fill the Sky"

Eternal God, Creator and Controller of the universe, God of power and might, God of gentleness and grace, God of second chances, we praise You in this Easter season for who You are and what You have done for us in Christ Jesus! Alleluia, amen! Christ is risen! Christ is risen indeed! Through him You redeem us, You reclaim us, You raise us from the earth and give us second birth, making us alive together with Him! Alleluia!

Forgive us when we forget this. Forgive when we doubt this. Forgive when we live fearfully because we don't trust Your abiding presence even in the darkest valley. Forgive when we get impatient with You, with each other, and with ourselves. Forgive when we get irritable and crabby. When we are ungrateful for what we have, while resenting others for what they have. When we turn a deaf ear to the poor, the powerless, the oppressed. Forgive. We confess these things openly. We ask that You help us repent. Wash and cleanse us. Remold and make us. Put in us a new and holy spirit. Hear now our silent prayers. (Silence.)

We ask Your blessings upon our loved ones; keep them safe, healthy, and happy. We thank You for Your generosity to us. Bless those who are burdened with grief. Give strength to the weak and hope to those who live in despair; give mercy to all of us when we sin. Help us use our influence faithfully and make us brave so that we may stand with those who are crucified with Christ.

We love You, Lord. We worship You! Let our praises fill the sky as we lift our hearts on high! Alleluia! And may our prayers never cease, even as we join now in the prayer Jesus taught . . .

"The Glory of Easter"

Thank You, O God, for the glory of Easter, and for its message that love triumphs over evil, that light overcomes darkness, and that life always pronounces the final word over death. We give to You our gladness and sing to You our praise. Christ is risen! He is risen indeed! To You be glory in the highest!

Forgive when we fall short of how You want us to live. Forgive our sins, our greed, our envy, our arrogance, our insensitivity. Forgive all that gets in Your way. Hear now our silent confessions. (Silence.)

Thank You for rooting and grounding us in Your love. Thank You for giving us patience for when we must suffer. Thank You for helping us persevere in prayer. Thank You for making a way where there seems to be no way. Thank You for forgiving our sins that we may be one with You: one living, life-giving body in You.

Thank You for setting us free from things that bind us that we may live unburdened and unafraid. Thank You for giving us eager spirits to be with You, and strong flesh to stay awake and watch. Thank You for Jesus, who was dead and is alive, and because He lives, so shall we!

Bless and keep our loved ones. Help us entrust them and ourselves into Your hands. Give us confidence in Your healing power. Grant us a lot of patience when we must wait without answers. Keep us equipped and close to Jesus, who came not to be served, but to serve. We pray for the homeless and the poor. For the sick and those who grieve. For those in recovery from addiction. For those in prison and those at war. For children who are bullied and need to believe in themselves, and for students who stand up for themselves and march, so that violence may end and that their classrooms may become safe again. Hear our silent prayers. (Silence.)

Thank You, O God, for the glory of Easter and its reminder that You love us always, Your unceasing light shines upon us, and Your resurrecting life lives within us to the end of time. All this we offer in the name of the risen Christ who still teaches us to pray together . . .

Pentecost

"Pray Like Never Before"

O God of love and life and joy and power, help us praise You like never before! We thank You! We proclaim Your loyal love in the morning, and Your faithfulness at night! You make us happy by all that You do, and we sing for joy! We adore You! We bless You! You are good and great and worthy of praise!

Pour out Your Holy Spirit once more. Cleanse and refresh us. Mold us, remake us. Forgive our sins, help us forgive ourselves, forgive our impatience with each other. Teach us again that no one is beyond Your redemption. Hear now our silent confessions. (Silence.)

We pray for our graduates. We are proud of their accomplishments; may they take pride, too. As You have given them knowledge and ability, equip and send them forth to serve and encourage others, and to seek justice and work for peace. We pray for our General Conference delegates who represent us. Anoint them with Your Spirit, that they may seek to better understand. Though there be difference of opinion, let there be oneness in Christ.

We pray for the sick, the poor, those in prison, and those at war. We pray for the oppressed and for those who grieve. We pray for the revitalization of our baptisms on this birthday of Your church, that we may continually rely upon Your Pentecostal power. These things we ask in the name of Jesus, who rose triumphant from the grave, and who still teaches us to pray together . . .

"On This Pentecost Sunday"

O God of Pentecost, we praise You for who You are: God of grace and glory; God of majesty and mercy; God of blessings; God transcendent over the universe, yet as intimately near as our breathing. You made us. You know us better than we will ever know ourselves. You love us even before we love You. You move in and through and among us before we ask.

Yet, on this Pentecost Sunday we ask for _____, we invoke Your presence, we invite You here. Come, Holy Spirit, like the wind Jesus spoke of when he talked of being born from above. Come as the fire at night that led Your people safely through the wilderness. Breathe on us; fall afresh.

Thank You for being a safe God with whom we can be vulnerable. Forgive us when we lose interest in You. Be patient when we don't like each other. Teach us how to forgive ourselves. Set us free when we are angry for childish reasons. Take us in again when we need a place to belong. Hear our silent prayers now as we open our hearts. (Silence.)

We pray for vacation Bible camp, for adults and youth faithfully employing their spiritual gifts for teaching and encouraging; we pray for the children, the many children, that they may have fun, and learn, and catch a glimpse of You.

84

Remind us, all, that life is good. Help us grow wise. Make us strong where we have been broken. Heal our wounds enough that we may practice wounded healing. Melt us. Mold us. Fill us with indignation when anyone is taken advantage of; use us to speak for those who have no voice. May we comfort the grieving, give counsel to those confused, and reassure anyone who is afraid. Let the fires of Pentecostal peace and hope shine through us. We pray in Jesus's name, the same Jesus who still teaches us to pray together . . .

World Communion

"Changing Gracefully"

O great Shepherd of our souls, in You we have everything we need. Thank You. Even in times of darkness and danger You help us walk unafraid. You feed us well. You lead us in safe places. You bring us home when we get lost. Thank You.

Thank You for the dear people we love, and yes, for people difficult to love. Thank You for those who encourage us when our world gets turned upside down and nothing makes sense. Thank You for being in our lives and letting us be in Yours. Hear now our silent prayers of thanksgiving. (Silence.)

Forgive us when we don't listen well, or when we say the wrong thing. Forgive when we want to strike back. Forgive when we think we don't need each other. Forgive when we make it harder for someone. Hear now our silent prayers. (Silence.)

We pray for those in need. Those who are grieving. Those who are oppressed. Those who need work. Those who need hope. Use us to help. Help us make hard decisions when we doubt ourselves. Help us speak the truth, but always with love. Help us when it's not easy to be patient. Help us when we face necessary change to change gracefully. Though our flesh is weak, give us Your Spirit, O God, that we may eagerly follow You through Jesus Christ.

We honor him today on this World Communion Sunday. Make us one with him and with our Christian sisters and brothers around the world. Unite us now as we pray together the prayer Jesus still teaches us . . .

All Saints Day

"All the Saints"

Eternal God, thank You for all the saints who from their labors rest, for the great cloud of witnesses surrounding us, a blessed communion. We rejoice in them as they rejoice in You. Grant us their faith to love You with all that is within, to confess You confidently before the world. Give us their courage to fight for You as they fought, to seek You first as they sought. Keep us humble, as you kept them. We name those dear to us silently before You now. (Silence.) Grant them your peace that perpetual light may shine upon them.

Draw us to Jesus, the same way the crowds were drawn to Him when he taught. Gather us so we may sit at his feet, look upon His face, learn from Him, enjoy him. Equip us with His Spirit and set us to work on Your purposes, that we may bear good fruit for You.

Help us rid ourselves of distractions that trip us, or slow us down, or hold us back. Shine Your light in our darkness. Cast out our fears. Wipe away our tears. Triumph over every evil that tempts us.

Hear our prayers for the sick, the dying, those at war, and for the victims of drive-by shootings and their families. Help us love those who don't love us; help us forgive those who do not have it in their hearts to forgive in return.

We pray in the name of Jesus Christ, the pioneer and perfecter of our faith, who endured the cross, who died and was raised that we might be raised with him, Alpha, Omega, the first, the last, the One who still draws us to himself and teaches us to pray together . . .

"Those Who Serve"

We praise You, God, from whom all blessings flow! We praise You for the beauty of the earth and the glory of the skies! We praise You for Your light and love and joy and grace, and best of all for the gift of Yourself!

Thank You for all the saints who now from their labors rest, and for the saints who still labor among us. Thank You for our country and our freedom to vote. Thank You for all those who have offered themselves to serve in public office. Bless them. They inspire us to be better informed and involved in the issues affecting us all. Hear now our silent prayers of thanksgiving. (Silence.)

May we think of each other as family, as Your children, as sisters and brothers who know that none of us is any more or less a part of Christ's body. We are different by Your design, and that is good. We have different personalities, different beliefs and gifts, and that, too, because You made us, is good. Help us treat each other respectfully, speak of each other honorably, especially when we disagree. Forgive us whenever we fail to do this. Hear now our silent prayers. (Silence.)

We pray for prisoners and those at war. For the poor. For the sick, and for those without health insurance. For those who have been harmed and now need a safe place, a healing space where their stories will be heard. For all of us who keep pushing back our tears, who haven't allowed ourselves to cry, but need to. Hear our silent prayers for all in need. (Silence.)

Keep us connected to You, O God, like branches to a vine. Scatter us like seeds on good soil, that we may bear abundant fruit for You. As we live, may we live *for* You. And when we die, may we die into You, knowing that, whether we live or die, we will always *belong* to You. We pray all this in the name of Jesus Christ, over whom death no longer has any power, and who still teaches us to pray together . . .

Special Days

Mother's Day

"For the Blessings of Home"

O God, You are our light and salvation. You save us from sin. You heal our brokenness. You restore us to right relationship with Yourself. You watch over our going out and our coming in. In You our hearts take courage. We praise You, and honor and thank You.

Thank You for the blessings of home, for our children, sisters, brothers, and dearest friends. Thank You for our dads and, today, especially for our moms. Thank You for their love and patience. Thank You for their faithfulness, tenderness, and compassion. Thank You for the way they did, and continue to do, their best to hold us accountable, that we may make them proud by the way we live.

We confess we fall short of the best persons we can be. Forgive us when we do things we regret. When we let someone down who counted on us. When we are not cheerful in serving others. Hear our silent confessions. (Silence.)

We pray for the sick and those who are grieving. We pray for those who are barely making it economically, and for those who are not making it. We pray for those who have been exploited or treated with cruelty. For those who frighten us, and for those whose needs we don't understand. Hear our silent prayers. (Silence.)

Open our hearts to You that we may give ourselves completely. Plant in us Your seeds of faith. Send us into Your harvest. Put us to work for You, unafraid, confident in Your name, Your Spirit, Your power. We ask it for the sake of Jesus, who died so that we might live, and who still teaches us to pray together . . .

"Those Who Have Shaped Us"

O God of our mothers and fathers, our grandmothers and grandfathers, we praise You. O God who reveals Yourself so completely in Jesus Christ who is our Alpha and Omega, who is, and was, and is to come, we worship You. O God who keeps us from falling, our only Savior to whom belongs glory, majesty, power and authority, we love You now and forever.

Thank You for those women and men who have shaped and formed us in so many good ways. They loved us. They saw potential in us. They encouraged us. They cheered for us. Bless them. Thank You for giving us the desire and determination to be like them. Forgive us when we think they have nothing more to teach us, that we are so much smarter. Forgive when we find it hard to forgive them for not being perfect. Hear now our silent prayers of gratitude and regret. (Silence.)

Thank You for reaching out over and over. Thank you, that when we fail to recognize You, You just keep trying. Thank You for coming to us in our times of exhaustion and renewing our strength. Thank You for quietly counseling us when we must make hard decisions. Thank You for rejoicing when we care for each other, especially when we imagine we are caring for You. Thank You for giving us compassion for the sick, those who have lost loved ones, those in prison, those who fear they will never be free from financial worry, and those who have knowingly been hurtful. Hear now our silent prayers. (Silence.)

We offer our prayers in the name of Jesus, who keeps reminding us that nothing can separate us from His love, not distress, nor danger, nor even our doubts, and who still teaches us to pray together . . .

"The People We Have and Those We Lost"

Happy the home, O God, when You are there! Happy the home when we remember how important You are. Thank You for always being there. Thank You for being You. Give us homes, Lord God, where You are known and loved and served. Give us homes where prayer and song and praise come naturally to every tongue. Give us homes where Your grace transforms us into new creatures in Christ.

As a mother or father has compassion for their child, so You, Lord, have compassion for us. You made us. We are Yours. We belong to You. You formed our inward parts. You knit us together in our mothers' wombs. You knew us before we were born. You loved us then . . . You love us now. And we love You.

Hear our prayers for mothers who have excelled at mothering. Bless them. Hear our prayers for mothers who have found mothering difficult. Bless them. Hear our prayers for women who long to become mothers. Bless them. Hear our prayers for mothers no longer with us. Bless them. Hear our prayers for mothers we never knew. Bless them.

Hear our prayers for those in need, those who are ill, those who are dying, and those who have entered Your joy in the life to come. Comfort those who are grieving, those who have been hurt, and those who find it hard to hope. We pray for the unemployed, the poor, those in prison, those at war. We pray for our planet earth, in all its beauty. We prayerfully rejoice with those celebrating new beginnings. Hear our silent prayers now. (Silence.)

We thank You, God, that we still have You, and always will. Forever. We worship and honor You this day as we pray again the prayer Jesus still teaches us to pray . . .

"Mothers Living and Dead"

We sing praises to Your name, O God, for You are great! Yours is the power and the glory and the majesty forever and ever!

Forgive us this day our sins. Have mercy on us when we do wrong. Give us repentant and obedient hearts. Wash us thoroughly. Cleanse us from regret and guilt. Fill us with Your all-sufficient goodness. Grant us right spirits and restore us to the joy of finding ourselves in You.

We pray this day for our mothers, those living, and those who have died and gone before. Bless and strengthen their love for us. Encourage their laughter. Comfort and reassure where they have known disappointment. Make Your face to shine upon them and keep them forever in Your grace.

Increase the influence of Your church. Pour out Your Spirit that we may dream dreams and see visions. Anoint us with compassion for those oppressed and hurting. Stir our commitment to justice and righteousness, that we may love them and practice them. Help us not be those who insist on our own way. Hear now our silent prayers. (Silence.)

Show us the path of life, O God. For we know in Your presence there is fullness of joy, our hearts are made glad, our bodies rest secure, and we enjoy pleasures forevermore. We know this through Jesus Christ who lived it, and died for it, and lives again that we might be one with You. We pray in His name, as He still teaches us to pray . . .

Father's Day

"Happy Fathers. Significant Men."

You are the God of our lives, and we love You! We come to worship You, to set our hearts and minds on You. We believe in You. We trust in what You say. We rejoice in what You do. You fortify us with the bread of life; You give us living water that never runs dry. You nurture us in our need and pull us to our feet. You are there through thick and thin, in every season, protecting our backs, building us up. You give us reason to shout, to dance, to laugh. You are the Creator of the universe and all that is in it: earth, sea, sky, and everything that has breath. You are greater than ever we can imagine. And You are our friend, and we do love You for that!

We also love the significant men in our lives. Our fathers, stepfathers and foster fathers, our grandfathers and godfathers. Our brothers of the same parent, our brothers in Christ Jesus. Thank You for Your grace that has come through them. Thank You also for difficult lessons we learn from some of those same men when relationships go wrong, and things don't work out well. Keep us humble that we may forgive, even as You forgive us. Hear now our silent prayers. (Silence.)

We pray for those who don't feel much love today. Those who have no home, no health. Those in danger. Those who have been hurt and don't understand why. Those to whom justice has been denied. Those who do not like themselves. Hear our silent prayers. (Silence.)

We lift our prayers to You, O God of love, in the name of Jesus, who called us His friends that we might all be one in Him, and who still teaches us to pray together . . .

"The Best That Is in Men"

O glorious and blessed God, Maker of heaven and earth, God of our fathers and mothers, and all those You have led in the past, hear our prayers. You are our ruler, our guardian, our guide, the One whose paths we make our own. Thank You for refreshing us, for keeping our hope new through Christ Jesus.

We pray today for our dads. Bless them as we do. May we understand, forgive, and honor each other. Thank You for the good ways You have influenced us through them. Thank You for the father figures who have mentored and coached and encouraged us. May the best that is in all these men be in us, and may we use it to bless future generations.

We pray for the poor and hungry. For those in the hospital and rehab centers. For the dying and the grieving, and those in prison. For public schools and community services and budget shortfalls. We pray for ourselves when we fall short and ask Your forgiveness. Hear our silent confessions. (Silence.)

Lord God, we love You and we love Your church. Thank You for what You have done through its ministries, and for what You promise yet to do. Use each of us to make a difference in somebody's life, and may the glory be Yours. We ask in Jesus's name, who still teaches us to pray together . . .

Independence Day

"Independence Day Approaches"

Eternal God—Creator, Redeemer, Sustainer—God of light, God of resurrection and hope, receive our worship and hear our prayers. We praise You for abiding with us. We praise You for being our help, You who never changes. We praise You for shining through our gloom and pointing us to the skies. In life, in death, O Lord, You abide with us. Thank You for reassuring our troubled hearts, that they may not be afraid.

With Independence Day this week, Lord, we give thanks for our country. We know we are richly blessed to live in the United States of America. Thank You for our Constitution; our Bill of Rights; and our government, which is of the people, by the people, and for the people. Thank You for our freedom as a nation. Correct us when we do not live up to our highest principles and bless us when we do. Keep us able to agree to disagree on important issues, while preserving an attitude of respect and generosity toward all.

We pray for those fighting wildfires, and for those who have lost their homes. We pray for those living in poverty, for the unemployed and the uninsured. We pray for those in prison, and those living in the midst of war.

We pray for loved ones who have died, and lift them up to You, O God. Keep them safe. Hold them always in the arms of Your mercy. Surround them with Your light. Embrace them in Your joy. We thank You for the times we shared, and the blessings we received because of them. We remember them before You now in silence. (Silence.)

Comfort us in our grief. Help us reach out in comforting ways to those who are grieving. Thank You for Your steadfast love that never ceases, for Your mercies that never come to an end and are new every morning. Thank You for continuing to abide with us, to tarry with us. We love You, God, and offer these prayers in the name of Jesus, our risen Savior and Lord, the One who still teaches us to pray together . . .

"American Interdependence"

Give us hearts to praise You, O God of all peoples and nations. Give us hearts full of grace and goodness that we may lift our hopes and dreams, our songs and prayers to You. Create in us clean hearts set free from sin, God of majesty and mercy, God of patience and peace. O give us hearts to praise You this day for Your love that raised Christ Jesus from the dead never to die again, from which nothing—not things present nor things to come—can ever separate us. We praise You, O God, through whom all things were created, and in whom all things hold together. To You be glory and honor forever and ever . . . this is our song!

O God, we bow before You as broken people. We have been hurt and we have caused hurt. We have allowed self-interest to take priority over other's interests. We have hoarded what we have and been hesitant to share. We are fearful of unknown outcomes and prone to expect the worst. We don't like people we don't understand. We really don't know how You can love us the way we are. Hear our silent prayers as we lift up our own needs and others in need. (Silence.)

As we Americans rightfully celebrate our independence as a nation, help us also acknowledge our interdependence with Your daughters and sons everywhere, and our ultimate dependence on You, in this life and the next. We ask these things in Jesus's name, the same Jesus who still teaches us to pray together . . .

"True, Just and Excellent"

Great are You, O God, creator of heaven and earth, and greatly to be praised! We honor You, we bless You even as we ask Your blessing. Thank You for our country, our home that we love. We celebrate all about it that is true and just and pleasing and excellent. Thank You for America, for its spacious skies and amber waves of grain. Thank You for being our God and loving us with steadfast faithfulness. We love You, and celebrate Your goodness, grace, and glory.

Thank You for the power and work of Your Holy Spirit in and among us. Thank You for Your church and electing us to its ministry. Thank

You for wisdom, and the courage we depend upon for the living out of these days.

We confess our fears and doubts. Too often, we give into evil thoughts and actions. Too often we rely upon our own strength instead of Yours. We too easily forget the poor and oppressed. We are too slow to provide comfort for those who are hurting and grieving, or those who are sick or in prison. Hear our prayers of silent confession. (Silence.)

Forgive us, Lord. Plant seeds of grace and mercy within. Make us patient instruments of peace. Help us listen more closely when we disagree that we may find new understanding. Help us lower our defenses, let go our insecurities, and allow Your love for difficult people to flow through us. All this we ask in the name of Jesus, our risen Savior who makes all things new, and who still teaches us to pray together . . .

"Spacious Skies and Amber Waves"

Our great and gracious God, we come to this place to worship. You make us one people with our sisters and brothers across the earth. We are a grateful people, hopeful, redeemed in Christ Jesus, firmly grounded and blessed by Your all-sufficient grace.

Thank You for our country, our home that we love. We celebrate all about it that is true and just and pleasing and excellent. Thank You for America, for its spacious skies and amber waves of grain.

Thank You for helping us get many things right . . . for holding fast to what is good, for doing our best to honor each other, for extending hospitality to strangers, for living peaceably so far as it depends on us, for rejoicing with those who rejoice and weeping with those who weep.

We also confess. We are too often fearful. We give in to evil thoughts and actions. We rely upon our own strength instead of Yours. We forget the poor and oppressed. We feel inadequate in caring for those hurting and grieving and sick and in prison. Hear our prayers of silent confession. (Silence.)

95

O great and gracious God, forgive us. Plant seeds of mercy within. Make us patient instruments of peace. Help us listen closely when we disagree that we may gain new understanding. Help us lower our defenses, let go our insecurities, and allow Your love for difficult people to flow through us. All this we ask in the name of Jesus, our risen Savior who makes all things new, and who still teaches us to pray together . . .

"Our Country, Our Home We Love"

O great and loving God, You created the heavens and the earth! We honor You. We bless You, even as we ask Your blessing. Thank You for our country, our home that we love. It has its challenges, but today we celebrate all about it that is true and just and excellent. Thank You for America, for its spacious skies and amber waves of grain.

Thank You for being our God, loving us with steadfast faithfulness. Thank You for the power and work of Your Holy Spirit in and among us. Thank You for Your church and electing us to its ministry.

We confess our fears and doubts. Too often we give into evil thoughts and actions. Too often, we rely upon our own strength. Too easily, we forget the poor and the oppressed, those who are hurting, grieving, or in prison. Too little of Your love has reached them through us. Hear now our silent confessions. (Silence.)

Forgive, Lord. Shed Your grace upon us. Help us lower our defenses and let go of our insecurities. Make us instruments of Your peace. Bless our brotherhood and sisterhood from sea to shining sea. Enable us to trust, that by Your work within us, You can accomplish abundantly far more than all we could ask for or imagine. We pray this in the name of Jesus, who makes all things new, and who still teaches us to pray together . . .

"The Freedoms We Enjoy"

O God, from whom all blessings flow, we bless Your holy name! O God of pure, unbounded love, we love You also. O God of abundant grace and overflowing tenderness, we adore You.

96

We thank You for our country and the freedoms we enjoy; help us not take them for granted. Thank You for providing our every need, and for sustaining our every breath. Thank You for the wonder of creation, for those dear to us, for safety and security and the certainty of Your Presence. We lift to You silently now our many thanksgivings. (Silence.)

We confess that not everything is well with us. We have sinned, and we have done that which is not pleasing to You. Forgive us. We are over-confident about what we think we know, but don't; keep us humble. We complain too much. We get angry too easily about things that happen, or that don't happen, and fault You for not stepping in. Hear now our silent prayers of confession. (Silence.)

We pray for the victims of shootings, and those who mourn. We pray for our leaders; may they lead honorably. We pray for anyone who is afraid. For those who don't have enough, and those who have too much. Hear, O God, our silent prayers for those in need. (Silence.)

O Joy of heaven, You are our God and we are Your people. We love You. We open our hearts with these prayers in the name and Spirit of Jesus, who is, and was, and is to come, and who still teaches us to pray together . . .

Election Day

"A Thousand Tongues Not Enough"

Lord, even if we had a thousand tongues to sing Your praise, it wouldn't be enough! All glory and power, all wisdom and might, all honor and blessing belong to You, with thanks never ceasing! You are full of wonder! You are great and grand! You are strong and beautiful! We praise You, we celebrate You, we rejoice in You! We barely have enough tongues to begin. Thank You for being here. We're glad You're glad we're here. Help us pray simply and well.

We give thanks for our country, for its freedom, its commitment to the well-being of all, its hatred of injustice. Protect it. Make it strong while saving it from false pride. Make its leaders wise, brave, compassionate.

Thank You for our veterans who served and who serve. May any injuries, physical and moral, be healed. Thank You for our democracy ensuring our right to vote. Remind us, regardless of the outcome of any election, our hope and confidence always lie in You.

We pray for each other that in all matters we may practice respect. May we comfort the discouraged, encourage the weak, and be patient with everyone. May we not forget those at war, or in prison, or the poor, or our elderly, all who too easily become invisible. Save us from self-doubt. Where our esteem has been wounded, give us new victories. When bad things happen, or we make mistakes, let us not allow them to define us. Keep our sense of humor fresh and our spirits light. Remind us that while weeping may linger for the night, joy comes with the morning. Hear now our silent prayers of petition and confession. (Silence.)

We lift our eyes to You, O glorious and gracious God, who brings life and health and peace, who sets us free from all that binds. Even if we had a thousand tongues to praise You, it wouldn't be enough. Receive these our prayers that we offer in the name of Jesus, who suffered, and died, and rose that we might live, and who still teaches us to pray together . . .

Veterans Day

"Those Serving and Those Who Served"

O glorious and blessed God, we rejoice, we give thanks with grateful hearts. We praise You, good and gracious God who is above, and through, and in us all. You created us and delight in how we are wonderfully made. We belong to You and in You we rest secure.

We pray this day for veterans who have served our country, giving thanks for their dedication and sacrifice. We give thanks for women and men currently serving. Protect them. Make them brave, make them wise. Instill in them Your higher calling to protect the innocent and seek liberty for those who are oppressed. Help us befriend and heal those veterans

98

and their families who are wounded physically, morally, spiritually, so that, in so far as it depends on us, we may live peaceably with all.

We know, Lord, when something hurts it hurts even more when we keep it closed inside. Give us courage to share our hurts with each other, and to turn them over to You. Help us cry when we need to, to grieve and be sorrowful, naming before You our regrets and mistakes. And where we have caused harm, make us quick to apologize, seek forgiveness, and repent. Hear now our silent prayers. (Silence.)

We love You, Lord. You are our strength. You are our rock, our refuge, our rescuer. Thank You for Your patience, Your understanding, and for Your abundant grace in Christ Jesus, which is sufficient. It's enough. It's all we'll ever need. In Your grace we can do all things, and we are learning to be content with whatever we have, even giving thanks with grateful hearts in all circumstances.

Hear our prayers, and unite us again in the prayer our Lord Jesus still teaches us to pray together . . .

"For a Veterans' Banquet"

Almighty God, Creator of heaven and earth, from whom we come, in whom we live and move and have our being, to whom we return when we die, You have been our dwelling place in all generations. You are our shield and shelter in the storm, our mighty fortress in danger, our refuge in times of trouble, the One in whom we place our trust. Thank You for being our God. May we be Your people who join You in seeking truth and justice, and people who stand with those least able to defend themselves.

Tonight, we pray for the veterans who have served our country, giving thanks for their dedication and sacrifice so that we may continue living in a land free from tyranny. We give thanks for the women and men currently serving our country. Protect and keep them safe. Make them wise. Fill them with compassion. Instill in them Your higher calling to protect the innocent and seek liberty for those who are oppressed.

Thank You for the veteran ministries of this congregation: providing care packages where they are deployed, keeping their names before us in prayer, walking alongside them and their families as they reintegrate into our communities, and listening to countless hours of their stories without judging.

Thank You for the small groups seeking to engage in "soul repair" through study, service, writing, and recreation. Thank You for all efforts to better understand and befriend those who are wounded physically, morally, spiritually. Thank You for planting in us the desire to become healers, to live in harmony, to seek what is noble, and, so far as it depends on us, to live peaceably with all.

Thank You for the food tonight that is before us in abundance, and for those who prepared it. Bless it to the nourishment of our bodies, and us to Your continuing service in the name of Jesus Christ, the One who saves, the One who serves, the One who makes us strong, and who fills us with joy. Amen.

Earth Day

"Vision, Wisdom, and Best Thoughts"

O God of grace and glory, hear our prayers. Thank You for our daily health and strength. Thank You for our loved ones, for food in abundance, for homes, for jobs, for our great nation. Thank You for the good earth and all that is in it, as we honor the beauty of Your creation on Earth Day. Thank You for Your church and help us become worthy of the ministry to which You call us. Thank You for being You and for revealing Yourself most completely in Jesus of Nazareth, the suffering one; the risen one; our Christ, who is rich in mercy, patience, and peace.

Forgive us when we are quick to take offense at another's words, swift to assume the worst about their intentions. Bless us when, instead, we look for the good, and initiate and nurture it. Forgive us for being our own worst critics and bless us as we strive to become our own best friends. Forgive us when we create distance between ourselves and You and bless us when we return to the embrace of Your arms. Hear our silent confessions, now. (Silence.)

Increase our compassion for those in need, especially anyone suffering pain, oppression, and injustice. Assure those who are grieving, and those who struggle with depression or addiction, that they are not forgotten.

Renew in us a passion for seeking out the lost, bringing back the strayed, and strengthening the weak. Help us work for that which is honorable, pure, and pleasing in Your sight. Be our vision, O God, our wisdom, and our best thoughts. Defend us with Your heavenly grace and, by Your Spirit, confirm us to eternal life. All this we ask in Jesus's name, the same Jesus who still teaches us to pray together . . .

"Let Heaven and Earth Praise"

Blessed are You, Lord God! We lift Your name on high! Let heaven and earth praise You, the sea and sky, the mountains and trees. Let all creatures of the ground and birds of the air praise You, for You are great and You are good!

Thank You for giving us eyes to see signs of Your creativity everywhere, and ears to hear Your voice deep inside. Thank You for Your Spirit to encourage and strengthen. Thank You for Christ Jesus dwelling in our hearts, rooting and grounding us in Your love.

Forgive our pride when we try to do too much ourselves, and when we worry too much about looking good in front of those we want to impress. Teach us again how precious we are to You, just the way we are. Forgive our disbelief. Forgive us when we drop the ball You would have us carry. Hear our silent confessions. (Silence.)

We pray for flood victims who have lost homes and livelihoods. We pray for victims of violence. We pray for the disabled, the poor and hungry, the refugee and outcast, for those who suffer mental illness. We pray for those who grieve. We pray for those who feel invisible, for those who feel they are a burden, and those who feel You have gone away. Hear our silent prayers. (Silence.)

O Lord, keep us humble, keep us civil, keep us close that we may walk before You in our integrity. We are Your simple people. We have little to offer but ourselves. Use us as Your witnesses, if You will. Lay Your hand upon us and give us words of grace. We ask in the name of Jesus who leads us in Your way, who embodies Your truth, who lives forevermore that we, too, may live, and who still teaches us to pray together . . .

"Caring for Creation"

Great God of the universe, maker of heaven and earth, we celebrate Your world! You call things that don't exist into existence. The air we breathe, the water we drink, the ground on which we stand. Light and dark. Plants yielding seeds and fruit trees bearing fruit. All living things, each according to its kind. You made it all out of love! You blessed and called it good! Receive our grateful praise! How majestic is Your name throughout the earth!

Thank You for molding us from dust, giving us form and texture. Thank You for our bodies. Help us delight in them, and in each other's physical uniqueness. We are Your children now and always, even when we forget or stop believing it.

Thank You for making us caretakers of Your creation. May we care for it well. Forgive us when we mistreat the earth. Forgive us when we pollute the air, water, and soil; forgive our excessive municipal waste, defoliation of forests, and overconsumption of natural and nonrenewable resources. Teach us to honor creation as You do. Hear now our silent confessions. (Silence.)

Hear our prayers for those in need. For the poor, the sick, and those who grieve. Those at war, and those in prison. Those who worry about money. Those who secretly suffer. Those who know they need to ask for help. Hear now our silent prayers. (Silence.)

We pray in the name of Christ who was in the beginning and part of everything that was made, who died and was raised so that all creation might be one in Him, and who still teaches us to pray together . . .

Memorial Day

"For Those Who Sacrifice"

Almighty God of the living and the dead, we give You thanks knowing whether we live or die, we are with You. We belonged to You before we were born, as now, and in the life to come. We pray on Memorial Day weekend for those who have loved and blessed and shaped us, and have now died and gone ahead . . . our grandparents and parents, sisters and brothers, spouses and dearest friends, our children, and those who have laid down their lives in the service of our country. We honor them on this day. We pray that we may be reunited with them in Your careful timing. Though we see them no more, help us never forget them, even as our memories grow dim. Let their rest be in Your shalom, and may the light of Christ shine upon them and embrace them always. We lift them to You now in silence. (Silence.)

Employ us, O God, to make peace. Some of us need help making peace with those who died. All of us need guidance in getting along with the living. When we are unsuccessful at love, at least help us agree not to do harm. Forgive us when we make matters worse. Use us to repair our small part of the world, and hopefully our good intentions will prove contagious. Help us encourage someone today, knowing even a little bit can change a life forever. Let there be peace on earth, dear Lord Jesus, and let it begin with us.

These prayers we offer humbly, also boldly. For we have tasted and seen how good You are! How wonderful, how marvelous! In Your grace our souls are made well. Make us well now, and one, as we pray the prayer Jesus still teaches . . .

"Those Gone Before"

O God, our God, Maker of heaven and earth, Redeemer of creation, Sustainer of all that lives, we worship You. O God of self-giving, compassionate, unconditional love, we adore You. O God in whose presence there is beauty, purity, harmony, and excellence, we praise You.

Time keeps passing and it seems like it is passing faster all the time. Here it is, Memorial Day weekend, once again. We remember the unpredictability and the blessedness of life. Thank You for those we love who have gone on before us. Thank You for those who gave of themselves and died in service to and for love of our country. Help us measure and treasure each day we have left to serve You that we may be found good and faithful.

Forgive us when we do things that in our better moments we would not. Forgive when we lose enthusiasm for following You because we have no vision. Forgive when we stop caring what happens to other people. Forgive when we hide from You, and please, dear God, remind us that it is always safe to come out. Hear now our silent prayers. (Silence.)

Hear our prayers for those who have been abused. For the poor. For those who are ill, and those whose hearts are heavy with grief. For those who are eager to work but cannot find jobs. For those who are estranged from each other. For those who struggle to love themselves. Hear now our silent prayers. (Silence.)

O God of grace and glory, receive our prayers. And please remember how much we love You even as You first loved us. All this we lift to You in the name of Jesus, who died, and is alive forevermore, and who still teaches us to pray together . . .

"Mighty, Majestic, Mysterious"

O God of pure, unbounded love, thank You for being *how* You are, and *who* You are. You are mighty, majestic, mysterious, yet You enter our world as an infant, becoming One with us, for us. You are utterly transcendent; You are the Creator of the universe, and yet You are intimate, ever available, and as close as our breathing. You give us Your law and commandments for our well-being, yet You are patient and understanding when we break them. Thank You, God; we praise You, God, for *how* and *who* You are.

Save us, O Lord, from any kind of impurity or greed. Protect our minds, guard our hearts. Do not let us stray, lest we fall into sin. Give us moral strength that we may control our urges. Make us swift that we may run

104

from temptation. Forgive us for what we did or failed to do this past week that got in the way of Your love. Hear now our silent prayers of confession. (Silence.)

We pray for the poor in spirit, that they may find hope. For those who mourn, that they may receive comfort. For those who hunger and thirst for what is right and just, that they may be fed until they are full. And on this Memorial weekend we remember and thank You for all those who have gone on before us in death this last year, and all who gave their lives in service to our country.

O God of pure, unbounded love, we lift our prayers to You in the name and Spirit of Jesus Christ, risen triumphant from the grave, who lives forever that we may live also, and who still teaches us to pray together . . .

"Whether We Live or Die"

Almighty God, we give You thanks knowing whether we live or die, we are with You. We pray on Memorial Day weekend for those who loved and shaped us, and for those who have now died and gone ahead: our grandparents and parents, sisters and brothers, spouses and dearest friends, our children, and those who have laid down their lives for our country. We honor them. We pray to be reunited one day. Though we see them no more, help us never forget, even as our memories grow dim. Let their rest be in You, and may the grace of Christ embrace them eternally.

Employ us, O God, as peacemakers who build and bring together. Some of us need help making peace with those who died. All of us need guidance in getting along with the living. When we are unsuccessful make us quick to confess and repent. Help us strive to do no harm. Forgive when we make matters worse. Use us to repair our small part of the world, and may our good intentions prove contagious. Help us encourage somebody today, knowing even one kind word can change a life forever. Hear now our silent prayers of confession and recommitment. (Silence.)

These prayers we offer humbly, gratefully, for we have tasted and seen how good You are, God of glory, Lord of love! In Your presence our souls are made well. Heal us now, and make us one as we pray the prayer Jesus still teaches . . .

New Year's

"Us and Everyone Else"

O great and mighty God, how majestic is Your name in all the earth! We praise and give You thanks. Your steadfast love endures forever. You watch over us every morning, every night, and in between. Thank You for becoming one with us again at Christmas, and for being our God all year long.

Thank You for health and strength, and for our hearts, lungs, and kidneys. Thank you for the blood coursing through our veins, for bones and muscles and skin. Thank You for medicine and medical care, for homes and heat and loved ones.

Thank You for Your comfort all year long when we have felt sad, and frightened, and insignificant.

Thank You for our consciences that keep us sensitive to the needs of others, and for our convictions to help where we can. Thank You for showing us in Jesus how to care for and love ourselves. Thank You for feeding us daily, O Bread of heaven, so we have all we need, and everyone else does, too, even our enemies.

Forgive us, dear Lord, when we doubt how close You are. Forgive when we think less of ourselves than You do. Forgive when You ask us to do something and we ask You to find someone else. Forgive us when You forgive us, but we won't forgive others. Hear now our silent prayers. (Silence.)

O great and mighty God, guide and watch over us. Keep us close, keep us out of trouble, and keep us in love with You all year long. We ask humbly in the name of Jesus, who still teaches us to pray together . . .

Prayers for Any Week

"God Yearns to Hear"

(From Jeremiah 29:10-14)

O loving and listening God, we worship You. We thank You for guiding us as we journey. Thank You for quenching our thirst and satisfying our hunger. For calming our anxious fears. For shining upon us with redeeming grace. For leading us in right paths. So many times this week, You've been there for us. Hear our silent prayers of praise and thanksgiving. (Silence.)

We confess our difficulty in getting along with each other. We think to ourselves, "Why can't everybody have the same opinion as me?" We become irritable, rude, prone to seek our own advantage. We are quick to condemn others and sometimes ourselves. We don't listen well. Lord, in Your mercy, hear our silent confessions. (Silence.)

Lord, show us what saddens Your heart. Help us see as You see. When we are in pain, or confused, or sad, or angry, or feeling defensive, it is hard for us to hear You. Teach us about ourselves in these stressful moments. Teach us how to love as You love. Teach us when we need to lighten up on our judgments against each other and against ourselves.

We pray for [*insert specific needs from your community and the world*]. For those grieving great losses. For those who need healing in body, mind, and spirit. For those homeless, and country-less, for whom there is no room in the inn. For those who feel they are not important and don't matter. Hear our prayers for those in need. (Silence.)

Thank You for treasuring these moments of prayer. So do we. We pray in the name of Jesus, who still teaches us to pray together . . .

"All the Time in Between"

(From Philippians 4:8)

O God of all creation, we worship You. We thank You for being with us at the very beginning of our lives, and at the end, and all the time in between. Thank You for being our strength and shield, and for the good work You do within us and through us. Thank You for good rest. For watching over our sleep and dreams, for guarding our hearts and minds. Thank You for teaching us to trust You. Give us the grace to trust You even more.

Forgive us for thinking too small. For thinking we're right, so that somebody else has to be wrong. For our impatience with ourselves. For impatience with You. Forgive us for taking our privileges for granted. Hear now our silent confessions. (Pause.)

We pray for those who have been hurt and those who know sorrow. For those who are ill, those infected with the coronavirus, and those overwhelmed with medical expenses. For those desperate for work. For those who hunger. Those whose anxiety is overwhelming. Those who struggle through the night without sleep. Those who fear the worst thing is the last thing. Hear our silent prayers for those in need. (Pause.)

Give us a tenderness toward creation. Help us forgive each other for poor decisions. Help us make peace with growing older, no matter our wrinkles and memory loss. Help us know what matters to You and then make it matter to us. Help us pursue what is excellent and admirable, what is true and holy, what is just and pure and worthy of praise.

We give You our prayers because You love us more than we'll ever know. We pray in the name of Jesus, in the power of Jesus's name, who still teaches us to pray together . . .

"Shine Your Light Through"

(From Romans 12:3)

Eternal God, we are here to glorify You, to tell of Your greatness and sing of Your grace. Thank You for the blessings of health, family and friends, our homes and country. Thank You for what You've done through the suffering, death, and resurrection of Jesus Christ, setting us free from all that would bind or prevent us from fully becoming Your people. Thank You for Your Spirit making us one with Christ, one with each other, and one in ministry. We praise and celebrate You, most holy God.

We confess to knowing of things separating us from You. Be patient with us. Forgive us when we relate to others as opponents rather than sisters and brothers loved by You. Forgive us when we take secret delight in the downfall of another. Forgive us when we think more highly of ourselves than we ought, and when we don't think of ourselves as highly as we should. Hear our silent confessions now. (Silence.)

Hear our prayers for those in need: those who suffer pain, those who are confused or feel lost, those whose hearts are breaking, those who are exploited by systems beyond their understanding, and those engaged in battles with evil and afraid they may lose. We lift them silently to You. (Silence.)

We humbly ask, O God, that You shine Your love through us. Like lamps on a hillside make us messengers of hope. We ask in Jesus's name, the same Jesus who taught then, and teaches us now, to pray together . . .

"Heal, Protect, Strengthen, Fight"

(From Psalm 92:1-4)

Great are You, Lord; great, and grand and good! Your glory is higher than the skies! Your name is praised from sunrise to sunset and through the night! You are God, and we worship You!

Thank You for the way You help us trust You. Thank You for the courage You give us when we are afraid. Thank You for Your presence even

109

when we are unaware. Thank You for Your counsel when we don't know what to do. Thank You for Your comfort when our hearts break. Thank You for Your grace when we find it difficult to forgive. We confess we take You and Your generosity for granted. Here now our silent prayers. (Silence.)

We pray for those who are ill. Heal them. We pray for those without homes who live in poverty, especially their children. Protect them. We pray for those who feel they are being tested beyond their abilities. Strengthen them. We pray for those who are oppressed. Fight for them. We pray for ourselves that we may grow increasingly faithful to Your kingdom and righteousness.

O Jesus who was crucified, who died and was buried, who rose triumphant from the grave and is alive forevermore. O Jesus Christ, be above us and beneath us, around us and within us. Be with us in all our circumstances, that we may be with You. We offer these prayers in Your name as we again join in the prayer You still teach us . . .

"To Be Used by You"

(From Isaiah 6:8)

O God, we have come into Your house to worship You. Splendor and majesty, strength and glory are Yours! We magnify Your holy name. Alleluia! Loud praise to Christ our King! With our hearts and voices, we sing!

Thank You for loving us and promising that nothing in all creation can separate us from Your love. We love You, too. Thank You for healing our broken spirits, for picking us up when we fall, for Your forgiveness when we sin, for steadfastly believing in us when we stop believing in ourselves. Grow in us grateful hearts that we may become wise, and generous, and full of courage.

Keep us eager to be used by You to bring grace into other people's lives. Wherever there is need—here we are—send us! We freely and heartily give You ourselves. Make us doers of Your word. Deploy us to heal our broken world. Use us to comfort the sick and those who grieve. Send us to visit the prisoner, to work on behalf of the poor, to stand with the oppressed. Make us one with our African sisters and brothers in Malawi [*substitute people or a group with whom your congregation has a relationship*]. You never said it would be easy to care, but You did promise it would be worth it! Hear now our silent prayers for those in need. (Silence.)

Make us teachable and willing to be changed. Enable us to see You and trust You in every situation. Keep our attention focused on You even as You keep drawing us to Yourself. We ask this through Jesus Christ, our refuge and strength, our light and salvation, and who still teaches us to pray together . . .

"Running for You"

(From Psalm 63:1-4; Isaiah 40:28-31; and John 11:38-44)

Almighty God, who we know best in Jesus Christ through the power of the Holy Spirit, to You we sing. You are ours and we are Yours. You love us and we love You. You are our light, our joy, our vision, and we pray to become part of Yours.

Forgive us when we act in ignorance. When our faith is faint. Forgive when we are careless with our words. When our sin leaves our souls sorrowful and sick. When we focus too much on ourselves and fail to focus on You. Hear now our silent confessions. (Pause.)

Lord Jesus, You are the One we've been waiting for, the One we need. We hunger for You. Where we are spiritually blind, give us sight so we can see as You see. Help us pray for each other as You pray, cry, and celebrate with each other as You do.

When we stumble and fall, raise us up on eagles' wings that we may soar for You and not grow weary. When we have that in our heart that is unclean, cleanse and heal us. When we are deaf and not hearing You well, open our ears that Your voice may be crystal clear. When there is that in us that is dead, unbind us and call us forth from our tombs. When we are poor in spirit and desperate for an encouraging word, preach to us Your good news of hope and grace. May we be of good use

111

to You today. We pray this in the name of Jesus who still teaches us to pray together . . .

"Won't Ever Let You Go"

(From 2 Corinthians 12:9)

We worship You this day, O God of all the nations. We have seen the light of Your glory. We know the hope that comes from Your salvation. We realize the healing power of Your name. Therefore, we praise You, Creator of heaven and earth!

Your persistent, steadfast love is something too wonderful for us to understand. You search us and know us better than we'll ever know ourselves and You love us still. We love You, too. We don't ever want to let You go. Teach us to love and keep loving.

Pour out Your Spirit that we may see Your visions and dream Your dreams. Mold our minds, warm our hearts. Give us ears to hear You, and conviction to follow. We celebrate the visions You have given our sisters and brothers in Malawi and Zimbabwe [*substitute people or a group with whom your congregation has a relationship*], and the dreams You've given us to join them in ministry.

Continue leading us to serve those without adequate schools or housing or transportation or employment. Give us big hearts for the sick, the grieving, and lonely. Teach us compassion, gentleness, and patience. Forgive our hesitancy and indifference toward anyone in need. Hear our silent prayers. (Silence.)

These things we offer in the strong name of Jesus Christ whom You raised from the dead, whose power is made perfect in our weakness, whose grace is sufficient for our every task, and who still teaches us to pray together . . .

"In Him All Things Hold"

(From Psalm 118:24 and Colossians 1:17)

We are here, O God, to speak glorious things of You, to give You honor—Father, Son, and Holy Spirit—ever three and ever one. This is the day You have made, Creator God; we rejoice in it and are glad. Your work is amazing—the beauty, the brilliance, the detail we see in a bird's feather, a cat's fur, a dog's personality, the petal of a flower. We are in awe at how Your sunlight glistens on an icicle. We are touched by Your uniqueness, majesty, and wonder. It makes us want to respond somehow, to pay tribute, to give back, to serve, to invest, to build something in Your honor, to say "Thank You" for who You are and how You are.

Hear our prayers of confession where we fall short of who You dream us to be. Forgive our insecurities, our slowness to believe in ourselves the way You do. Comfort us in our loneliness. Strengthen us in our weakness. Embrace us when no one else will. Forgive our impatience, our criticalness, our hesitancy to love as You love us in Christ Jesus. Keep us mindful of others whose needs are as legitimate as ours—the need for safety and health, and peace, and justice, and hope. Hear the silent prayers we lift now for ourselves and for all Your people. (Silence.)

You have made Christ our sure foundation, our head and cornerstone. In Him all things hold together. In Him we find our adoption and redemption. In Him we experience Your good pleasure and the riches of His grace lavished upon us. In Him we find faith, and reassurance when we lack faith. In Him is the beginning and the end of our lives, the Alpha and the Omega. In Him we find rescue from the power of darkness and entry into Your kingdom of light. In Him You put Your mighty power to work by raising Him from the dead and making Him chief over all things for the church, which is His body. In Him we have everything we need. In Him we praise You, and through His living Spirit we pray now, again, the prayer he still teaches us to pray together . . .

"Oneness and Wonders"

(From Hebrews 12:1-2 and Matthew 5:14-16)

O God of oneness and wonders, we stand in awe of what You do. How do You do it? You bring light into our darkness. You overcome our separation, making us one with each other and reconciling us to Yourself. You heal our wounds and forgive our sins. When we mess up our lives You restore us to our rightful place as Your daughters and sons. You make us one in heart and one in spirit. We praise You, O God! We love You, O God!

Forgive us when we forget how important You are to us. Forgive when we forget how important we are to each other. We often disagree and either fight or avoid. We lose patience. We become condescending. We misunderstand. We stop trying. Forgive us when we get ourselves into the wrong place. Hear now our silent prayers of confession. (Pause.)

Hear our prayers for those who are hurting. We pray for survivors of trauma. For those wrestling with addiction. For those in prison. For our neighbors housed and unhoused. For the hungry that they may be filled, and the ones who weep that they may laugh. For those who do not yet know love. Hear now our silent prayers. (Pause.)

Help us run the race You set before us, keeping our eyes fixed on Jesus. May we be of good use to You today. Make us salty. Make our light shine so as to draw attention to You. O God of oneness and wonders, thank You for doing what You do and being who You are. We worship You. We love You. Unite us again now as one body in the name of Jesus who still teaches us to pray together . . .

"Teach Us to Think"

(From 2 Corinthians 5:17-20)

Almighty God, Your grace is truly amazing. The sound of it is sweet. We keep getting lost, and You lead us home. We stumble in the dark, and You give us Your light. We fall in the dust, and You wash us clean. We praise You! We praise You!

We confess that we have allowed distance to come between us and You and each other. Forgive us for saying things we don't mean and forgetting to say things we do. Forgive us for taking each other for granted, and for being emotionally unavailable when we are together. Forgive us for being slow to seek reconciliation where there has been harm. Hear now our silent confessions. (Silence.)

Thank You for Your transforming work. Thank You for teaching us to think, and see, and hear in new ways, for helping us imagine saving possibilities. Help us invite Christ to live within, to become new creatures in Him, to fall in love with Him. Grow us, mature us, draw us closer to Yourself in Jesus. Help us believe in Him that we may have life in His name and live in eternal union with His Spirit.

We pray for the poor, those in prison, those who grieve. We pray for those who are oppressed and those who are at war. We pray for those in need of healing, and for our planet that suffers from neglect. We pray for our country's leaders. Help them build bridges. We pray for other nations. Help us better appreciate our differences.

Hear these prayers we lift to You because of what Jesus has done, and who He is. Amazing grace, how sweet the sound. Unite us now in His continuing prayer . . .

"Keep Us Sensitive"

(From John 14:15-18 and Matthew 28:20)

O God, we worship You. We praise You with our whole being as long as we live! We praise You for the beauty of Your creation. For Your faithfulness. For giving justice to the oppressed, sight to the blind and straightening those who are bent low. For Your strength. For Your protection. We praise You!

Thank You for revealing Yourself in Jesus. When we lose our direction, we get reoriented in Him. When we forget our purpose, we find it again in Him. When we get fuzzy about who we are we rediscover ourselves in Him. When we feel distant from You, He's the one who reminds us You are as close as our breathing, and You love us too much to leave us alone.

115

Keep us sensitive like Him. Forgive us when we cause hurt. Help us know when to reach out and when to back off. We never know what prior hurtful experiences each other carries. Help us learn from our mistakes. Give us courage to apologize. Make us humble enough to receive apologies. Grant us mercy always and hold us in Your grace. Hear our silent prayers. (Pause.)

We pray for those who are sick and for those in pain. We pray for those who need a good cry. And those who do not forgive themselves. For those who cannot sleep. For those troubled about death. For those who need a friend. For those learning that You specialize in healing broken hearts. Hear our silent prayers. (Pause.)

Thank You for listening and for loving us so much You will never leave us alone. We pray in the name of Jesus who bids us follow, and who still teaches us to pray together . . .

"We Worship, We Commit"

(From Joshua 1:5-9 and Galatians 5:22-26)

We bless You, O Lord. We worship Your holy name. When the sun comes up every morning—no matter what will happen throughout the day—it's time to sing, like never before, a song to You and worship Your holy name.

We worship You for the way You calm our fearful anxiety, reminding us: "Fear not, I am with you." We worship You for the way You lift us when we are weak that we may stand strong. We worship You for the way Your grace proves all sufficient when we pass through fiery trials, supplying our every need. We worship You for the way You keep us humble, receive our confessions, and absolve our sin.

We worship You for the way You enable us to love ourselves and our neighbors. Hear the prayers we offer on behalf of the sick, the grieving, the discouraged, the hungry and homeless, and those in prison. We pray for our sisters and brothers in [*name locations of war and unrest in the US and world*] and everywhere there is warfare and strife. We pray that all children may be free from harm, kept safe and warm, that they may grow happy and whole. Hear now our silent prayers. (Silence.)

We worship You by recommitting ourselves—our work, our play, our financial resources, our influence. We commit ourselves to slow down, be still, and know You are God. We commit ourselves to seek and bear the fruit of Your Spirit—love, joy, peace, patience, generosity, gentleness, self-control. We commit ourselves to live and be guided by Your Spirit, and to belong forever to Christ Jesus, crucified and risen.

We bless You, O Lord. We worship Your holy name. We lift our hearts gladly and joyfully, knowing that it is You who made us and that we are Yours. Receive our prayers in the name of Jesus, who still teaches us to pray together . . .

"Saved, And So We Serve"

(From Ephesians 2:4-10)

O great God, Maker of heaven and earth, You are excelling grace, our crowning joy. You create us anew, restore us afresh, rebirth us from above. You save us from sin that we may faithfully serve. You are the strength in our weakness. You are the light on our path. We glory in Your perfect love.

Thank You for giving each of us the power of influence; guide us in using it justly and with compassion. Thank You for the courage to face our fears. Thank You for reminding us we don't have to prove ourselves to You. Thank You for helping us endure gracefully when we are misunderstood or rejected. And when we dig ourselves into holes, thank You for helping us climb out.

Forgive our over-sensitivity and self-criticism. Forgive when we are so focused on ourselves that we don't see You. Forgive when we hold back from who You want us to be. Forgive when we become comfortable with the suffering of others. Hear now our silent prayers. (Pause.)

We pray for the hungry and homeless, for those in prison, and for those at war. We pray for the sick and those who have heavy hearts. We pray

117

for those who can't find a decent job, and for those who are miserable in the jobs they have. Hear now our silent prayers. (Pause.)

We glory in Your perfect love. We pray in Your perfect name, the name of Jesus who came to encourage, to challenge, and to break bread with us, that we might be one with Him and each other, and who still teaches us how to pray together . . .

"Like Those Who Walked with Jesus"

(From Matthew 4:18-22)

Come, Thou Almighty King, help us Your name to sing, and to praise, and to bless. Blessed are You, O Lord our God, Ruler of the universe, Creator, Redeemer, Sustainer of all that was, and is, and will be. Come, Eternal One, and reveal Your glory and power among us. Come, Lord Jesus: our Alpha and Omega, our way, our truth, and our life.

Bowing in Your holy presence we are impressed with a sense of our sin and how we daily separate ourselves from You by thought, word, and deed. Like those who walked with Jesus, who fished with Him, and who humbly bowed and prayed in His presence, we, too, acknowledge our brokenness and make our silent confession before You. (Silence.)

Grant us Your mercy. Wash and make us clean. Remove our fear and hesitation. Restore us as forgiven and forgiving people. Search us with Your eyes, smile upon us and speak our name. Come this day to our seashore and free us to leave our nets and follow. Take possession of our hearts that we may be instruments of peace toward the poor, the captive, the blind, the oppressed, the forgotten.

Help us bring good news to somebody, to encourage as You encourage. We can do nothing without You, and more than we can imagine with You. Make us so completely Yours that it is no longer we who live, but You who live in and through us. All this we pray in the name of Jesus, who still teaches us to pray together . . .

"Losing Enthusiasm"

(From Acts 18:24-28)

We love You, God. We love You for who You are. You give us life, so that our hearts beat, our lungs breathe, our muscles flex. You heal us when we are broken. You overcome everything that tries to separate us from You. You sustain us with Your patience and power. Come, creator God. Come, redeeming Christ. Come, Holy Spirit. We love and adore You.

Forgive when we lose our enthusiasm for following You. We get distracted, discouraged, enduring only for a while. Forgive when we resist Your grace for reasons we don't understand. Maybe because we don't think we're worth loving? Forgive when we fail to hear the voices of those crying out for help because we're too absorbed in ourselves. Hear now our silent confessions. (Pause.)

We pray for the poor. For those who live with pain. For those who live with violence. For those working for justice within our communities, who need to be encouraged and celebrated. For those trying to fix things that cannot be fixed, who need a dose of reality. Hear our prayers for those in need. (Pause.)

Thank You, O God, for being who You are. Thank You for working in and through us the way You do. We love You. Thank You for helping us trust Your good timing, and to embrace Your promise to be with us to the end of time. O God of infinite possibilities, we ask these prayers in the name of Jesus who was crucified, who is risen from the dead, and who still teaches us to pray together . . .

"How Can We Thank You Enough?"

(From Psalm 8)

O great God, creator of heaven and earth and sea and sky, the moon and stars and galaxies, and all that is in them, and Who saw that it was good, how can we praise You enough? Who are we that You pay us any attention at all? Yet, You crown us with Your glory! You honor us by becoming one with us, giving Yourself to us, loving us. How can we thank You enough?

We try to live the way You want us to live. We try to honor the glory You have placed in each of us. Thank You for helping us do it well much of the time; we couldn't do it without You. Forgive when we fail the rest of the time.

Forgive, gracious God, when we forget to respect each other. When we grow short on patience, when we are jealous, or arrogant, or seek our own advantage. When we keep a record of complaints, when we deny justice, when we pull apart that which You put together. Hear now our silent prayers of confession. (Silence.)

We pray for the poor, those in prison, those who live with addictions, those who are oppressed. We pray that all children may grow up healthy and happy and whole, enjoying every advantage they deserve. We pray for our elderly, that they may receive adequate care and protection.

O great and enduring God, how can we praise You enough? You are who You were, and You still do what You did. Keep us in love with You. Help us love and honor each other, and ourselves. Teach us to persist and endure. We ask in the name and Spirit of Jesus Christ, who is completely One with You, who came not to condemn the world, but to save it, and who still teaches us to pray together . . .

"Losing Faith and Face"

(From Mark 4:35-41)

Lord, we love You, we worship and adore You, God of glory, God of grace. Thank You for being with us even in the storms. Even when we become fearful, losing faith and face, You are there. Always, You work for our good. We don't always see it easily at the time, but looking back we do. Thank You, thank You. We do believe in You; help our unbelief. Help us trust You more. Don't let what's happened to us—the good and the bad—go to waste.

Please forgive us for not thinking about You as often as we intend. Forgive us for not loving others as You have loved us. We fail to come to You with open hearts and hands. We need Your guidance, but don't ask. We need Your strength, but sometimes we focus on how tired we are. We know You are available in the present moment, but we stay stuck in the past and worry about tomorrow. Hear now our silent prayers of confession. (Silence.)

Forgive and restore us. Wash and cleanse us. Let us hear Your joy and gladness in us again, that we may live with new, steadfast, and willing spirits. Send us as Your servants to bring good news to the poor, release to captives, sight to the blind, and freedom to those oppressed. We ask in the name of Jesus, the same Jesus, risen triumphant from the dead, who still teaches us to pray together . . .

"Come From, Live In, Return To"

(From Psalm 139)

O God, our Creator, we come from You, we live in You, we return to You, Maker of heaven and earth. You are good! Your creation is good! We are good, for You formed our inward parts and knit us together in our mothers' wombs that we might be fearfully and wonderfully made!

We praise You for our bodies, hands, and feet. We praise you for our eyes, ears, minds, and for our voices that let us speak and sing and laugh. We praise You for the light of day and the dark of night; for clean air to breathe and safe water to drink; for warmth when it is cold and shade in the heat; and for grass, trees, flowers, birds, and bees. Let all things their Creator bless!

Forgive us as we confess our lack of nurture for what You made, for neglecting self-care, for minimizing the hurts of others. Teach us to love the earth the way You do. Help us go easy on ourselves. Forgive us that we worry so much and trust You so little. Show us how to honor the beauty we discover in each other, and the strangeness. Give us big hearts for the sick, the grieving, the poor, those in prison, those who suffer oppression, and remind us that their need for healing and justice and mercy is as urgent as our own. Hear our silent prayers. (Silence.)

We pray, O God, in the name of Jesus Christ. May He dwell in our hearts through faith. May we be rooted and grounded in His love. May we be filled with all Your fullness according to the riches of His grace. May we know Him and the power of His resurrection. May we become His reconciling body, a new creation made visible and available, beginning here today, in this place, as He still teaches us to pray together . . .

"You're Still Here"

(From Luke 12:22-32)

Thank You, God, for giving us life. We do love You. As needy children look expectantly to their father or mother for what they need, we look to You.

Where there's heaviness in our heart, lighten our burden. Where we're in trouble and sinking fast, rescue us. Where we are haunted by past mistakes, set us free. Where we have sinned, forgive. Hear now our silent prayers. (Pause.)

Help us grieve, honoring our sadness and tears. Nurture us when we don't feel like eating. Calm our anxieties when we are beside ourselves with worry. Soothe our spirits when we cannot sleep. Refresh us that we may again taste Your goodness and grace. And for those who don't yet know You, help them recognize You by what they hear and see in us. Hear now our silent prayers. (Pause.)

Help us see You everywhere: with the brokenhearted, the crushed in spirit, the sick in bed, the mourners at graveside. Help us remember Your presence among those locked in prison, those huddling under a bridge, or hiding from an oppressor's fist. Help us see You in each other, even those who *are* not like us, and those who *do* not like us. Breathe in us, and every time we forget Your nearness, nudge us gently with a smile and whisper, *I'm still here*. You've led us in the past, O God of our ancestors. Lead us again today.

We pray in the name of Jesus, the author and perfecter of our faith, who endured the cross, who gives us eternal life through his resurrection, and who still teaches us to pray together . . .

"Making Us Strong and Sensitive"

(From John 14:12)

Holy, holy God, to You be glory and praise for everything You do, and for who You are! Almighty! Merciful! Perfect in love! We rejoice in You! Let the earth hear our voice!

Thank You for making us strong—in body, mind and spirit—stronger than we think we are. Help us tap into that strength with great confidence that we may do what You would have us do. Thank You for helping us communicate, giving us just the right words to say what You would have us say. Thank You for helping us love ourselves as much as we love our neighbors. May we never doubt the goodness You put inside. Hear now our silent prayers of thanksgiving. (Pause.)

Thank You for keeping us sensitive to those who have been hurt and are being hurt. Give us courage to resist evil, standing up for others and for ourselves. Forgive us when we are short-tempered. Forgive us for the grudges we hold. Forgive the sins we must live with that haunt us. Forgive us when we fail to forgive others. Life's too short. Hear now our silent prayers of confession. (Pause.)

Hear our prayers for the sick, and those unable to communicate. For those suffering addiction or substance abuse. For those who have lost a pregnancy, and those going through divorce. For those who struggle to pay the bills. For those who have gone to war and died, and those who survived and are trying to make sense of what happened. For all our loved ones we have lost this year.

Holy, holy God, hear our prayers. We offer them in the name of Jesus Christ whose grace is sufficient, whose power is made perfect in our weakness, and who still teaches us to pray together . . .

"Too Crazy to Be Without You"

(From Mark 2:17)

Almighty God, Father, Son, Holy Spirit; Creator, Redeemer, Sustainer; God of wisdom, passion, and strength, we praise You! For our health and salvation, for life and breath, and for Your goodness and mercy, we worship You!

We need You. Our lives are too crazy to be without You. So many things are changing, and it's hard not to feel threatened. Sometimes it seems the harder we work at our relationships, the more tangled up they get. We try hard to respect the differences in each other, but it's not easy. We are too dependent upon our own resources, and not enough on You. Forgive our slowness to seek You. Forgive when we hurt each other. Forgive us when we are unwilling to forgive ourselves. Hear now our silent prayers. (Pause.)

We need Your help in praying for the poor, those in prison, those who live with conflict. We need Your encouragement that we might encourage the sick, the grieving, and those who feel like giving up. We need you to make us brave enough to be available to those who need help. Hear our silent prayers. (Pause.)

Thank You for being here. Thank You for making us unafraid. Thank You for lifting us when we fall. Thank You for Your surprises. Thank You for the laughter and hope You put in our hearts. Thank You for filling us with Your Spirit, that we may be of good use to You, till Your work on earth is done. These things we pray in the name of Jesus, who calls us his friends and who still teaches us to pray together . . .

"Too Smart for Our Own Good"

(From Philippians 2:5-13)

O God, You are grand, and glorious and good, from sunrise to sunset and all the time in-between. Your creation cries out its praise. Your redeeming work brings us to our knees in humble gratitude. Your sustaining Spirit lightens our hearts and fills us with joy.

Thank You for placing in us a desire for Your will, for growing us up into Christ, and for comforting us in His love. Thank you for uniting us in Your good works and calling us according to Your purpose. We do love You, Lord.

Help us not worry so much, and to trust You more. Forgive us for sometimes being too smart for our own good, and for undervaluing our worth. Please understand when it's hard to remain positive, and when we're quick to take offense. Correct us when our indifference causes harm. Cast out our fear. Cleanse us from sin. Hear now our prayers as we pour them out to You in silence. (Pause.)

May the mind that was in Jesus be in us. How quickly he reached out to the poor, the sick, the prisoner, the enemy. How willingly he welcomed the stranger. How he delighted in the laughter of children and blessed them, that they might prosper. How he bid us to set the oppressed free. May the same mind that was in Jesus be in us.

We lift our prayers to You, O grand and glorious God, as those who have been raised from death to life by the One who still teaches us to pray together . . .

"Seed, Soil, and Sun"

(From Luke 8:4-15)

We come before You, O God, with joy and thanksgiving. You are a great God! The mountains, and the sea, and the earth, and the sky are Yours. We praise You with heart and voice, for as long as we have breath, Lord Almighty, King of creation!

God of seed, and soil, and sun: help us be steadfast sowers for You. God of storm, and wind, and waves: help us be still and not fear. God of justice for the oppressed: help us join in Your work. God of mercy and grace: let our anger be slow and our love abound. God of compassion for those who lose their way: make us good guides providing wise counsel and glad news of deliverance.

125

O Spirit of God who raised Jesus from the dead, dwell within. Give us life. Put to death our sin and everything separating us from You. Free us from all that binds. Lift us when we fall. Forgive where we are wrong. Work in us Your goodness. Help us trust You more. Hear now our silent prayers. (Silence.)

We pray for those we love. Keep them safe. Surround them with Your light. Fill them with Your joy. We remember the sick, the grieving, the poor, and those with pressing need. Grant to all Your saving help. May those who seek You, find You.

We offer these prayers in the name of Jesus Christ, the pioneer and perfecter of our faith, who still teaches us to pray together . . .

"For Horses, Monkeys, Cats, and Dogs"

(From Genesis 1:31)

O glorious and blessed God, Maker of heaven and earth, God of our fathers, God of our mothers, God of all You have led in the past, hear our grateful prayers. You are our guardian and guide. Thank You for refreshing us with love and grace divine.

We pray today for our dads whether they are living or whether they have died. Bless them. May we honor and forgive each other. Thank You for Your influence through them, and for father figures who have mentored and encouraged us. May the best that has been in all these men be in us.

We pray for everyone who grieves, especially in Orlando, Florida [*insert a specific place, or pray simply for "everyone who grieves"*]. Comfort and bring healing where hearts have been wounded and covenants broken. We pray for the poor, the sick, those in prison, those living with addictions. For public schools, community services, and budget shortfalls. We ask Your forgiveness where we have failed to love neighbor and self. Hear our silent confessions.

We thank You, O Lord, for creation. For sun and moon, for wind and water and trees and sky and earth. For living creatures of every kind: robins, cardinals, and great blue herons. For fish and turtles and sea lions and whales. For horses and monkeys and cats and dogs. Help us respect creation and work to protect it. Teach us through each of Your creatures Your steadfast love and loyalty, and how to enjoy life light-heartedly. We ask in Jesus's name who loved creation, who lived, served, died, and was raised for creation's sake, and who still teaches us to pray together . . .

"Try to Say It Better"

(From Ephesians 4:29 and James 1:19)

O grand and glorious God, we worship You with our spirit and integrity. We praise You with open hearts, uplifted hands and voices of gladness. O good and generous God, in You our souls rejoice and our bodies rest secure.

Thank You for being patient and full of grace. When we're stuck in a place we don't want to be, help us make the best of it. When we try too hard to be liked by others, help us relax into the uniqueness of who You created us to be. When we don't like changes happening around us, help us keep our displeasure from spilling out onto others. When we say the wrong thing, and someone feels hurt, help us be quick to say, "I'm sorry. Let me try to say it better." In Your understanding and grace, O God, hear now our silent confessions. (Pause.)

Hear our prayers, O Lord, for those who suffer pain, and those oppressed by violence. For the unemployed and uninsured, and for those who make decisions about their lives. For those who work hard, but feel they have little to show for it. For those hungry for relationships where they can be understood, and where they can understand. For children, that it may be well with them; for their parents, that they may be steady and strong; for their grandparents, that they may be calm and wise.

Make us quick to call upon You, O God, in our every need. Touch our hearts and minds with glimpses of Yourself. Use us for Your purposes and keep us from getting in the way of what You're doing. We pray in the name of Jesus, who is risen from the dead; who was, is now, and shall be evermore; and who still teaches us to pray together . . .

"You Believe in Us"

(From Isaiah 43:1-4)

O God of good news, for us and all the world: You give us light, and hope, and joy! We praise You. We worship You. We love You.

Thank You for believing in each of us. Thank You for Your generous grace, loving us better than we'll ever know. Thanks for helping us pass that grace toward others, praying it makes a difference in their lives. And please, help us receive some of that divine grace into our own hearts—a bunch of it—especially when we have fallen short of Your love and need Your forgiveness. Hear now our silent prayers. (Pause.)

Thank You for those who challenge the way we think, though at the time we don't always appreciate it. They help us see possibilities we may not want to see, and somehow, we think You are involved in this. Move us away, O God, from jealousy, from judging, from name-calling. Let there be no home for hate here in Your house or in our hearts. May Your pure light, and Your mercy, flow through us.

We lift up to You those who are sick: heal them. Those who are sad: comfort them. Those who have done wrong: convert and restore them. Those who are in dangerous situations: protect them. Those who are searching for work: employ them. Those hungry for hope: feed them, as well as all the others in need, whom we name silently before You now. (Pause.)

Hear our prayers, O God of good news. We believe in You. Thank You for believing in us, and for working within us to accomplish abundantly far more than we can ask or imagine through Christ Jesus, who still teaches us to pray together . . .

"You Know What We Mean"

(From Romans 8:26)

O gracious and generous God, we love You. We love You for loving us. You came in Jesus and through His grace, His healing power and forgiveness, You draw us close to Yourself that we may all be one. For this we will worship and praise You forever. Thank You, thank You, thank You.

Forgive us when we get in the way of Your love. When we know the good, and intend the good, but don't do it. When we know the wrong, and intend to avoid the wrong, but do it anyway. Forgive us when we feel superior. When we are always looking for someone to blame. When we do not practice honesty. Hear our silent prayers of confession. (Pause.)

We pray for those whose lives are being turned upside down due to storms, floods, fires, and earthquakes. For the sick, the dying, the grieving, and those at war. For those desperate for a safe home for their families. For those who don't seem to care whom they hurt. For those who find hope and then lose it again. For those who are trying to find their place in the world. Hear our silent prayers for those in need. (Pause.)

We're not always sure, God, how best to pray. But we're trying. And we're trusting that You know what we mean. Teach us to pray with the confidence of innocent children who look to You for their every need. We ask in the name of Jesus, who delights in giving us his interceding Spirit, and who still teaches us to pray together . . .

"No One Like You"

(From 1 Chronicles 17:19-20)

O God, You are our refuge, our shelter. You protect us from danger. You rescue and deliver us when we're in trouble. You are our rock, our solid foundation on which we stand. Storms may come against us, but we are not overwhelmed because You are with us. You save us! We trust You. We depend on You. You are our continual hope, and we praise You as long as we have breath.

Forgive us when we doubt You. Forgive us when we worry too much, and when we forget that You are alive and working in and through us. Forgive us when our thoughts and actions get in the way of Your love for those around us. Hear now our silent prayers of confession. (Pause.)

Life is not easy, O God. So, we pray for those who struggle to pay the bills. For those who are separated from loved ones. For those who are afraid to die and those who aren't sure they want to keep living. For those who disappoint us and those who make us proud. Hear now our silent prayers. (Pause.)

This is Your day, Lord. You made it. We rejoice and are glad in it! Our souls long for You. We hunger and thirst for You. There is no one like You. You are our God, and we belong to You. We love You, and we will praise You as long as we have breath. Receive our prayers as we bring them before You in the name of Jesus, full of grace and truth, and who still teaches us to pray together . . .

"Bright Hope for Tomorrow"

(From John 8:31-32)

O great and faithful God, we worship You. For Your unchanging love, Your unending compassion, we praise You. For daily strength and bright hope for tomorrow, we glorify You. For the way You cheer and guide us, and bless us every morning and every night, we honor You.

We confess we are not the people we want others to think we are. We're not always sure who we are, or who we want to be. So, give us courage to surrender our lives to You. Mold us. Make us into the daughters and sons You've always dreamed we might become.

We confess we've done wrong. Grant us grace so as not to repeat it. Release us from prisons of our own making—our insecurities, our addictions, our prejudice. Free us to love, to trust, to forgive. Break our bondage, renew our minds, change our hearts. Hear now our silent prayers. (Pause.)

We pray for those who hunger and thirst. For those who suffer pain. For those who cannot sleep. For those who have died and for those who miss them. For those who cannot find work. For those who will not ask for help. For those in danger.

O great and faithful God, no matter how dark things get, we know Your love always wins. You bear with us, You believe in us, You hope through us, You endure because of us. Receive our prayers today in the name of Jesus Christ, who restores to us the joy of Your salvation, who is and was and is to come, and who still teaches us to pray together . . .

"Where We Can Make a Difference"

(From Psalm 139 and Matthew 25:34-36)

Dear God, we thank You. We pray joyfully because of Your becoming one with us in Jesus. Thank You for all You accomplished in His life, suffering, death, and resurrection.

You started a good work in us through Him, a work that promises to bear fruit. You search us, and know us, and lay Your hand in blessing upon us. We cannot go where You are not. Even when surrounded by darkness, we know the darkness is as light to You.

We pray for those in need of Christ's ministry: the poor, the ill, the grieving, those in prison, the oppressed, and those who oppress them.

We pray for those struggling with addictions, with financial debt, with unemployment. We pray for our challenged relationships with friends, spouses, children, parents. Help them, help us, dear Lord. And where we could have helped make a difference but didn't, forgive us. Hear our silent confessions now. (Silence.)

Thank You for Your grace. Thank You for believing in us. Thank You for making us stronger and more hopeful than we could ever be without You. Each time we remember what You do for us we feel closer to You. We feel reassured. We find ourselves loving You even more. May the goodness You pour into us move us to extend goodness to somebody else. We ask this in Jesus's name, who still teaches us to pray together . . .

"Increase Our Strength of Soul"

(From Ephesians 2:16-19)

We worship You, O God, all glorious above; we gratefully sing of Your power and love. We worship You with gladness. We come into Your presence with singing. You are God! You made us. We belong to You and no one else. You are good! Your steadfast love—wide and long and high and deep—endures forever. Your faithfulness extends to all generations.

We worship You just as we are. We open ourselves to You, exposing our good and bad. We are proud; we are embarrassed. We have done well; we have missed the mark. We want Your acceptance; we need Your forgiveness. We offer our gratitude; we make our confession. We surrender all that is in us, praying that, by doing so, we may discover true peace in You. Hear now our silent prayers. (Pause.)

We also worship You by lifting up the needs of others. We pray for all who are in troubled relationships. For those struggling to pay the bills. For those needing a successful interview. For those trying to get pregnant. For all who live with cancer. For all who grieve. For those coping with dementia and those who need a reason to keep living. For all who have no one else to pray for them.

We worship You, O God, by bringing our prayers—for You, for ourselves, for others. Thank You for Your abiding Spirit that enables our prayers and intercedes on our behalf. Increase our strength of soul. Fill us with Your fullness. Let us be employed by You, that we may bear pleasing fruit, fruit that will last. We ask in the name of Jesus, crucified and risen, who still teaches us to pray together . . .

"Even As You Know Us"

(From John 3:16-17)

Eternal God, our Savior and Shepherd, our Guardian and Defender, You have claimed us as Your own. We are Yours and You are ours. Blessed God, may our oneness never end. May we spend eternity together. Let us stand before You face to face one day and know You fully, even as You have always known us.

Increase our awareness of Your presence now. Help us trust without anxiety, leaning into Your strength. Help us enjoy You. Help us become the women and men You designed us to be. Let Your Spirit live in us and let us live in Your Spirit. Keep us close, that we may closely follow.

Lord, we know You have high expectations and hopes. Sometimes we let You down, we let each other down, we let ourselves down. We're sorry. Hear now our silent confessions. (Pause.) Thank You for Your understanding, Your patience, and Your grace.

And thank You for helping us get it right much of the time. When somebody's sick or discouraged or in prison and we visit. When we see the poor and befriend them. When people are exploited and there's violence and we do what we can to stop it. When we see an enemy and pray for them, or a stranger and get to know and welcome them. When we see children and delight in their play and laugh with them. Thank You, Lord, for helping us walk in Your ways.

Yes, we want to spend eternity together. But we'll be so grateful if for today You simply lead us where You want us to go. Direct our steps toward what You have prepared. We ask in the name of Jesus, whose name is above every name, who died and rose that we may live with Him, and who still teaches us to pray together . . .

"Gratitude and Regrets"

(From Isaiah 9:2 and Psalm 133:1)

O great God, Creator of the universe, who is born to us at Bethlehem, You are God, and You alone! Upon us, a people who walked and lived in a land of shadows and deep darkness, Your light has shined! You give us new birth into a living hope, and for this we praise and worship You!

Thank You for daily health and strength. Thank You for our loved ones, our dear friends, and those we're coming to know. Bless and watch over them. Thank You for Your encouragement. Thank You for

133

Your steadfastness. Thank You for Your presence and guidance when we stand helpless before threatening situations not knowing what to do or which way to go. Thank You for granting us Your calm in the midst of uncertainty. Hear now our silent prayers of thanksgiving. (Silence.)

May we never forget those on the streets without jobs, without protection, and too often without hope. We pray for children who are alone and afraid. We remember those in prison, those at war, and those living with addictions. We pray for the sick and those who grieve. We pray for families where there is misunderstanding, hurt, and reluctance to communicate. We pray that You save us from our sin that clings so closely and weighs us down. We pray that You keep safe our secrets we're not yet ready for anyone else to know. Hear now our silent prayers. (Silence.)

Thank You for Your mercy and grace. Keep us open to Your Spirit, and receptive. Give us a willingness to work hard for the well-being of others, making earth look more like heaven. We ask in Jesus's name who still teaches us to pray together . . .

"When We Do Not Ask"

(From Matthew 11:28-30 and James 4:2-3)

Eternal God, Creator of heaven and earth, You make us in Your image, You redeem us when we miss the mark, You renew and sustain us with Your Spirit each day. O dear and precious Lord, hear our prayers.

What if we asked You to lead us when we got lost? What if we asked You to help us stand when we fell? What if we asked You to strengthen us when we were tired, and weak, and worn? What if we asked You to show us the light when we were in the midst of a storm? What if we took Your hand and asked You to lead us home? O dear and precious Lord, forgive us for not asking.

What if we turned to You when we were afraid, and asked for courage? What if we turned to You when we were close to despair, and asked for hope? What if we turned to You when we found ourselves becoming angry and critical of others, and asked for patience and understanding?

134

O dear and precious Lord, forgive us for not turning to you and asking sooner. Hear now our silent prayers. (Silence.)

Hear our prayers for those who have died, and those who grieve. For those who are ill, and those whose memories are fading. We pray for the unemployed, for refugees, and those at war. We pray for those who serve as leaders in our institutions and in our government.

Make us instruments of peace and nonviolence. Build us up in Christ Jesus for good works. Knit us together as one with all those You love. Precious Lord, take our hands and lead us. We offer these prayers in Your name as You still teach us to pray together . . .

"The Forgotten Good Parts"

(From Psalm 118:23-24 and Mark 9:24)

This is a day, O God, to celebrate You! This is a day to praise You, a time to rejoice in You! You created heaven and earth and all things good. You breathe life into us every day. You sustain us in hard times and celebrate us in success. You bless us with family, friends, and those who are no longer strangers.

Thank You for setting us free from trying to be who we're not. Thank You for reminding us of the good parts of ourselves we had forgotten. Thank You for bringing Yourself alive in us in ways we never experienced before. Thank You for making us sure of You. Hear now our silent prayers of thanksgiving. (Silence.)

Forgive us when we lose faith, when we find it hard to trust. Forgive when we feel like quitting on the things You ask us to do. Forgive when we let our defeats define us. Forgive us for believing everything bad we hear about somebody on TV, or when we refuse to listen to those with whom we disagree. Hear now our silent confessions. (Silence.)

We pray for those who struggle to set healthy boundaries, and to keep them. We pray for those who live with pain, those wrestling with addiction, and those at war. We pray for our loved ones who have died, and for that part of ourselves that died with them. Help us cast our fear and anxiety on You because You care, and You can transform it. Stretch our faith muscles. Use us to bless and to bring healing to others. Lay Your hand upon us and give us words of grace. We ask this in the name of Jesus, who overcame rejection, suffering, and even death, and who still teaches us to pray together . . .

Notes

Introduction

1. "In U.S., Decline of Christianity Continues at Rapid Pace," Pew Reasearch Center, October 17, 2019, https://www.pewforum.org/2019/10/17/in-u-s-decline-of-christianity-continues-at-rapid-pace/.

2. "1. Religious and spiritual practices and beliefs," Pew Reasearch Center, August 29, 2018, https://www.pewforum.org/2018/08/29/religious-and-spiritual-practices-and-beliefs-2/.

1. Guiding Principles for Prayer-Writing

1. Dietrich Bonhoeffer, *Life Together* (London: SCM, 1954), 63.

2. *The United Methodist Hymnal* (Nashville: The United Methodist Publishing House, 1989), 870.

3. "John 14:13," Ellicott's Commentary for English Readers, https://biblehub.com/commentaries/john/14-13.htm, accessed June 9, 2021.

3. Delivering the Prayer

1. Kevin McSpadden, "You Now Have a Shorter Attention Span Than a Goldfish," *Time*, May 14, 2015, https://time.com/3858309/attention-spans-goldfish/.

Notes

Introduction

1. Jo Ellis, "Decline of Christianity Continues at Rapid Pace," New Research and Center, October 17, 2019, https://www.pewforum.org/2019/10/17/in-america-the-decline-of-christianity-continues-at-rapid-pace.

2. J. L. Brignoni and others, practices and beliefs," New Research Center, August 24, 2017, https://www.pewforum.org/2018/08/09/religions-and-spiritual-practices-and-beliefs/.

1. Guiding Principles for Prayer-Writing

1. Dietrich Bonhoeffer, The Psalms (London: SCM, 1982), 45.

2. The Daily Walk with Charles Wesley (Nashville: The United Methodist Publishing House, 1990), 870.

3. John 14:14, "Ellicott's Commentary for English Readers," https://biblehub.com/commentaries/john/14-14.htm, accessed March, 2021.

3. Delivering the Prayer

1. Kevin McSpadden, "You Now Have a Shorter Attention Span Than a Goldfish," Time, May 14, 2015, https://time.com/3858309/attention-spans-goldfish.